EMERGENCY VEHICLE OPERATION INSTRUCTION

5 Steps to Enhancing Your EVOC Training

Hugh Anderson

EMERGENCY VEHICLE OPERATION INSTRUCTION: 5 Steps to Enhancing Your EVOC Training
www.evoctrainer.com

Copyright © 2020 Hugh Anderson

ISBN: 978-1-77277-350-7

All rights reserved. No portion of this book may be reproduced mechanically, electronically, or by any other means, including photocopying, without permission of the publisher or author except in the case of brief quotations embodied in critical articles and reviews. It is illegal to copy this book, post it to a website, or distribute it by any other means without permission from the publisher or author.

Limits of Liability and Disclaimer of Warranty
The author and publisher shall not be liable for your misuse of the enclosed material. This book is strictly for informational and educational purposes only.

Warning – Disclaimer
The purpose of this book is to educate and entertain. The author and/or publisher do not guarantee that anyone following these techniques, suggestions, tips, ideas, or strategies will become successful. The author and/or publisher shall have neither liability nor responsibility to anyone with respect to any loss or damage caused, or alleged to be caused, directly or indirectly by the information contained in this book.

Publisher
10-10-10 Publishing
Markham, ON Canada

Printed in Canada and the United States of America

Table of Contents

Dedication	vii
Foreword	ix
Acknowledgements	xi
About the Author	xiii

Chapter 1: How I Got Started — 1
- A Mechanic's Son — 3
- Teaching Friends — 4
- A Race Car Driver? — 6
- The Day I Applied to Become a Licensed Driving Instructor — 8
- Meeting My Supervisor Instructor — 10

Chapter 2: The Early Years of Training — 13
- The Dichotomy of Racing and Safe Driving — 15
- Does Practice Make Perfect? — 17
- Invitation to the Police Academy — 19
- The Need to Prove Oneself — 20
- Why Can't They Drive? — 22
- Fun With Cone Courses — 23

Chapter 3: Mistakes That I've Made — 27
- Failing to Respect Learning Styles — 29
- What Do You mean, "It's Not About Me?" — 30
- Instructor Showboating — 32
- Slowing Things Down, Speeds Learning Up (Scaffolding) — 33
- Relaxing in the Front Seat (Never Wear Red) — 35

Chapter 4: Lessons Learned — 39
The Importance of a Plan — 41
Training for the Student, Not the Instructor — 43
Bridging the Track to the Road — 44
Patience Is Key — 46
The Importance of Non-EVO Training — 47

Chapter 5: Cone Courses and Track Training — 49
Seating Fundamentals — 51
Student Engagement — 53
Time vs Accuracy — 54
Good and Bad of Creating Competition — 55
Competence vs Confidence — 57
False Sense of Safety — 58

Chapter 6: Four Stages of Competence — 61
The Psychology of How We Learn — 63
Stage 1, Unconscious Incompetence — 64
Stage 2, Conscious Incompetence — 65
Stage 3, Conscious Competence — 67
Stage 4, Unconscious Competence — 68
Applying This to Your Training — 70

Chapter 7: Foundation of Expert Driving- Eye Placement — 73
Do We Really See With Our Eyes — 75
Importance of Peripheral Vision — 77
Tunnel Vision — 78
Correlation Between Speed and Vision — 79
Looking Through the Corner — 80
Proper Scanning Techniques — 81

Chapter 8: Commentary Driving	**85**
What Is It?	87
How Does It Work?	88
Bottom-Up vs Top-Down Processing	89
Benefits of Commentary for the Driver	91
Benefits for the Instructor	91
Language Matters	93
Chapter 9: Decision Making	**97**
Mitigating Driving Risk	99
Decision Making Model N.R.A. (Action Criteria)	100
Is It Necessary?	102
Is It Risk Effective?	103
Is It Acceptable?	105
Incorporating NRA into Training	106
Benefits of Incorporating NRA	108
Chapter 10: Training in Live Traffic	**111**
Driving – The Most Dangerous Thing	113
The Aura of an Emergency Vehicle	114
Feedback via Unsuspecting Motorists	117
Training in the Real World	119
Scenarios	120
Timely Instructor Communication	122
Epilogue	125

Dedication

I wrote this book in honour of my parents, Gail and George, neither of whom would have been surprised to learn that it took me so long to get this book to print, but I'm certain that they both are very proud.
XO

Foreword

I first met Hugh Anderson when he joined my Monthly Mentor program in 2006, and I quickly realised that this was a man who had a thirst for knowledge and a passion for training. It was obvious that Hugh was on a path to greatness within his chosen field and it has been fascinating to see just how far he has come over the years.

I thought that I knew my fair share about driving and, more importantly, teaching someone to drive, until I looked at this book and thought – wow, I don`t really know that much. *Emergency Vehicle Operation Instruction* documents Hugh's expertise and leadership in his field, with his primary focus being Train the Trainor for a great many years. In this book, Hugh has the ability to make the Art of Instruction come alive as he puts you inside the vehicle along with him, drawing upon numerous examples from his repertoire. His distinctive position as a specialist in police vehicle operations and his 25 years' experience within the driver training field provide for a unique perspective that will go a long way towards inspiring you to elevate your techniques when instructing emergency vehicle operators. Hugh's authentic writing style will cause you to pause for moments of reflection as he takes you along the journey of his career.

Having written well over 100 books and committed my own life to teaching, I can honestly say that I was astounded to see just how important the psychology of training and development is for emergency vehicle operations. Hugh's approach to incorporating the Four Stages of Competence and Decision Making criteria will undoubtedly open your mind to applying information to unique circumstances, thus enhancing your own training techniques.

Emergency Vehicle Operation Instruction

Personally, I had never really thought about applying these techniques to driver training, but Hugh takes an insightful look at what helps motivate you, whether you are a driver or a trainer. It's clear through this book that Hugh has the necessary knowledge and skills to be an excellent guide and mentor. His successful strategies and tips will prove to be both practical and relevant. This book is a must read if you are someone who instructs emergency vehicle operators, and wants to take your training to the next level.

Raymond Aaron
New York Times Bestselling Author

Acknowledgements

I would like to thank my wife, **Donna**, for encouraging and supporting me throughout this entire book writing process. I'm sure that she must have felt like a single mom at times as I spent countless hours sequestered in the basement. I would also like to thank my stepchildren, **Mitchell** and **Layla**, for teaching me to look at life through a different lens. You both have (unknowingly) taught me a great deal about life and about myself. Thank you, **Donna,** for inviting me to be a part of this family.

To my sisters, **Kimberly** and **Melody**, I thank you for putting up with me when we were young; I'm sure that I was a brat on occasions, and I know that I could be a royal pain... Thank you for looking out for me and supporting me throughout my career and life.

I am extremely grateful for my friendship with **Brad** and **Stacey Davis**. From the early days at the College, or my first day at Peel, the two of you have been in my corner. Our conversations, debates, and friendship are priceless. Words alone cannot express my thanks to both of you.

I can't say enough about the support and mentorship that I have received from **Jerzy Kwiatkowski** over the last 25 plus years. From the day that I met you, in 1993, until now, you have been a big supporter of mine. Thank you for the fellowship and conversations, which have always been insightful.

I would also like to thank **David Seal** for being able to put up with me during a tumultuous time in our careers at Peel. I am proud that the two of us were able to bring two separate groups together and develop them into one fine team.

I would also like to thank **John Mepham** for being a staunch supporter of mine. I have come to recognise that he has just as much passion for training as I do. He, however, has a much more diplomatic approach to getting things accomplished.

It wasn't until about the last six years or so, that I began to understand the importance of character and leadership within a training environment. For this, I have to give a great deal of thanks to **Ken Delaney** for helping me discover what a true leader looks like—Ken epitomises great leadership.

Within the first few months of my career at Peel Police, I had a lot of self-doubt on whether I had made the right decision to join this organization. I was fortunate to have met **Marg Abbot,** who worked in the Training Bureau as an administrative assistant at that time. She was very patient with me and helped me understand the bureaucracy surrounding organizations like this. Thank you Marg; I wouldn't have stayed at Peel if it wasn't for your calming influence and guidance.

I had the opportunity to see **Gordon Graham**, in Austin, TX, many years ago. In that presentation, I realized that one person really could make a difference if they dedicated themselves to Officer Safety, and to risk mitigation in general. It was refreshing to see that someone agreed with me that "if it's predictable, it's preventable." Thank you, Gordon, for helping me to recognize that my mission is not futile.

Who knew that a guest gig as an instructor at the Ontario Police College would lead to such a long and fruitful career for me? Had it not been for the awesome team of Police Vehicle Operations (PVO) Instructors that I worked with from 1998–2000, I would never have lasted. Thank you for being patient with the newbie, and for letting me absorb all of your knowledge though your combined experiences— they have proven to be invaluable. I learned so much during this time, and I still miss the camaraderie that we experienced as a team. I am not going to list the 20–25 individuals who helped me develop as a PVO Instructor, because I most certainly will inadvertently miss a name or two. All of you know who you are—a great big thank you to the **PVO Instructors of 1998–2000.**

In my search to find quality training for our team of instructors, I stumbled upon the Ohio Peace Officer Training Academy (OPOTA), and **Jeff Eggleston.** From the first time that I attended OPOTA, I knew that I had found a trainer who was also a visionary and was in sync with my training philosophies. His crew of instructors were varied, but they had also adopted a learning philosophy about training, and were open to other teaching strategies when it came to Officer Safety. Thank you, Jeff, for not only introducing me to your crew but, more importantly, for your friendship.

Many years ago, we took an unprecedented step in bringing a keynote speaker to our organization to discuss training—more specifically, paying for someone to speak about Driver Training within Law Enforcement. There was this little known Captain (now Major), from Tulsa PD, who would occasionally write something that would appear online. "Let's try and get him!" We did, and I am very pleased to say that **Travis Yates** agreed! Thank you, Travis, for inspiring me to not give up the good fight!

My career in Driver Training would have been much shorter had it not been for **John Le Feuvre.** John was the first person who showed me that training could be fun, and that innovation was much needed when it comes to Driver Training. Thank you for believing in me and demonstrating the value of being entrepreneurial and unique.

When I received a call to meet **Stephen Sturgess** for dinner, to discuss joining Peel Police, I wasn't sure what to expect, and I don't think he was either. The hiring of a Maverick! Thank you for believing in me and allowing me the opportunity to express my passion for training.

A few years back, my mind was opened up to the value of incorporating an action criteria model into driver training. **Scott Redstone** is a huge proponent of the NRA Action Criteria, and I thank him for not only helping with the "Decision Making" chapter, but also for his fellowship over the years.

During my time at Peel Police, I have had the opportunity to work with well over 25 trainers who have spent some time within the PVO office. From the nuances of processing a call, to how to deal with management and everything in between, you have taught me more than words can describe. Most importantly, I have enjoyed the day-to-day interactions as we continue along this path together. To all the current and past **PRP PVO Instructors**, thank you! Listing the names of each person, and telling a story for each, could be a book in itself, so I will save that for your retirement speeches.

I am also grateful for everything I learned while working at the Skid Control School, and would like to thank **Doug Annett** for pushing me to be a better instructor every day.

I have saved the most important people until last: **my students**. Thank you for allowing me the opportunity to help you become the best driver that you can be. I hope that you were inspired in some small way to be better. Please be safe out there!

About the Author

Hugh Anderson lives in Burlington, Ontario, Canada, with his wife and two stepchildren. He continues to work for Peel Police, where he fills his role as *Specialist – Police Vehicle Operations*.

The author is available for delivering keynote presentations to appropriate audiences, and to conduct Train the Trainer courses and/or workshops. For availability, please contact the author directly at: Hugh@evoctrainer.com.

To order more books, search for Emergency Vehicle Operations Instruction, on Amazon.com.

Also, if you would like to stay up on current information, would like to see the bonuses for this book, or to learn more about additional training opportunities, please visit evoctrainer.com.

Finally, if you have been inspired by his book, please pass this information on to the future generations of Emergency Vehicle Operators, so that they, too, can remain safe!

Chapter 1

How I Got Started

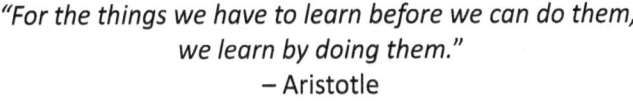

*"For the things we have to learn before we can do them,
we learn by doing them."*
– Aristotle

A Mechanic's Son

"Where did my love for driving come from?" you might ask. Growing up we didn't have a great deal of money, but my parents always managed to rent a waterfront cottage for two weeks every summer. One of the amenities that was a must-have, was the use of a tin boat, with either a 6hp Johnson or the sleek- looking 7.5hp Mercury. This was my happy place. From the time I woke up until the time I went to bed, all I ever wanted to do was drive that boat. Many mornings, I would wake at 6 a.m. to go fishing with my dad. Truth be known, I hated fishing but loved driving the boat. Around the time when I was 8 years old, I met a neighbour who had a minibike—we became fast friends. We went everywhere together, either on his minibike or in my boat. At the time, no one really cared if two eight-year-olds were tearing it up on the cottage roads or were jumping waves solo in a tin boat. My dad had only two rules: wear a life jacket, and stay in sight of our cottage—and all was good.

Emergency Vehicle Operation Instruction

My father was a mechanic who had his garage in the back of our yard, where I learned a great deal of things. Most importantly, I grew to hate smelling like grease, oil, and most definitely hand cleaner! I did, however, offer to help him, in the hopes that he would let me drive the vehicles into the garage or around the corner to our other driveway. By the time I was 11 years old, I was quite proficient at working the clutch, on the hill outside of the garage. Full disclosure here: I may have hit the door or work bench on an occasion or two. While helping at the garage, I came to the realization that not all people approached their car—or driving for that matter—in the same way. Some people were complete slobs, with garbage filling every door pocket, and over-stuffed sun visors and filthy windshields, while others were very fastidious as to how they kept their cars. The same went for how it looked on the outside. I remember one woman saying not to mind the scrapes on the door as long as it opened and closed... I have come to lean that people approach the driving task itself with pretty much the same degree of attention some are meticulous in their approach while others don`t give it a second thought once they`ve obtained their driver's license.

Teaching Friends

I received my learner's permit on my 16th birthday and had my full license within three months. Once I received my driver's license, I would offer to drive anyone anywhere, which enabled me to have the family car. Being the youngest of four drivers, and having only two cars at the house, I often found myself driving my grandmother to the grocery store, doctors, or church. If someone needed to go somewhere, I would always offer to drive. This is what allowed me to garner my driving experience— basically, I was an unpaid chauffeur.

Toward the end of high school, I was able to buy my first car. It was a fixer-upper and needed a great deal of work. It was the ugliest colour that you could ever imagine—Seafoam Green—but I was thrilled to call it my own. Since many of my friends were without a car, I was their driver; but this did have some unexpected benefits, most notably seldom having to pay for gas myself.

In grade 12, I had a friend who had just bought a Toyota Corolla with a 5-speed, and he had no idea how to drive it. One day, we walked to his house and took his car out for a drive, with me behind the wheel. Unbeknownst to me at the time, this is where my driver training career really began. After just a couple of hours of training, my friend was off and running with his Toyota, as his ability to operate a standard vehicle quickly evolved.

For the next few years, I spent quite a few hours teaching people how to drive standard. Now, if you've ever had the opportunity to teach someone how to drive a standard automobile, you know that it can be quite nerve-racking. Perhaps you can relate to the following: A friend of mine managed to back her car out of her driveway with me sitting beside her, but instead of clearing all the lanes of traffic, she managed to stop the vehicle on an angle, impeding traffic travelling in both directions. It had to be at least six or seven attempts before we got moving again, as she continually stalled on every attempt. Unfortunately for us, the traffic continued to build up, with someone ultimately sounding their horn in frustration—if they were frustrated, just think how frustrated I was! My friend was driven to tears, and we had to pull over almost immediately after clearing the lanes. We can look back now and laugh about that day, but it was very stressful at the time; and as an instructor, you know who she was blaming—yep, it was my fault.

Another training session that helped in my career was when I was helping my cousin learn how to drive her sister's standard automobile. We had pretty much grown up together and, at this time, I was in my mid-20s, and she had just begun her new career as a teacher. I drove her car out to a quiet country road, demonstrating the Hendon starting technique, and then we switched spots, allowing her to take the wheel. She actually took to it quite well; however, after about 20 minutes, we arrived at a stop sign, where there was a little bit more traffic. Once again, she got nervous and struggled with moving the car smoothly from the stop. The car did move, just not with a great deal of grace and/or smoothness. She was very upset that she had not mastered the skill of operating a standard shift car, and she stated, "How come I can't drive this car as good as you?" I asked her to pull over to the side of the road, and then I stated, "You are a very good typist; how many words can you type in a minute?" She told me that she can type 60 plus words per minute. "Wow, that's amazing; can you take me home and teach me to type at 60 wpm by dinner?" She immediately broke out into laughter, recognizing her absurdity in thinking that she would be able to drive a standard shift car as well as I could, after only 2 hours of practice.

A Race Car Driver?

It's interesting to me that as I look back on my driving, and ultimately my training career, I recognize that some very critical learning points, from which I draw upon, occurred in my early years of driving. One of them that stands out to me was the very first time that I took the family car, a 1974 Chevrolet Caprice Classic with a 400 small block engine, out on the highway for the first time, with my two best buddies.

We were on the highway, with the tunes all cranked as we travelled 10 minutes down the road to the next city, thinking that we were the coolest three guys in the world. I signaled our exit and began to slow down, but I realized that I was going too fast. Quickly thereafter, I noticed the Holiday Inn on the other side of the ramp—in fact, I noticed the open blinds in the window. (Time out; you are hoping that I am going to mention something fun going on in the room, but I'm sorry to disappoint—as an EVO instructor, you know what's wrong.) I was going through a sharp turn on this ramp, and I was simply looking at what I was about to hit! Yes, my car wasn't tracking very well, and I was lucky enough to reduce speed and make it through the curve. It wasn't very pretty, and my two friends were singing my praises and laughing hysterically; but in reality, all three of us knew that we had almost died—or at the very least totalled the car.

I know that an advanced driving instructor shouldn't be admitting to these mistakes, but to be honest, it was a great learning experience from which I draw upon quite frequently, especially when I am training in the art of proper cornering techniques.

As a teenager, I loved watching Formula 1 races, along with Indy Car; and in fact, any TV show with cars would always capture my attention. Very early in my academic career, my parents knew that I wasn't going to be a strong candidate for either college or university life. It was all that I could do just to get through high school. Thank goodness for football and hockey, and of course, my Building Construction classes. It was in these classes that I can say that I met a teacher who, for the first time in my life, I could call a mentor. My BCC teacher took a shine to me, as he recognized that I had some decent skills. In fact, he asked two of us from his class of 30 to help him build his own home during one summer. That was a great experience, as grade 12 was coming to an end, and it was becoming decision time for high school students as to what lies ahead. One conversation, which I will never forget, happened between me and my BCC teacher in the hallway. He took me aside and, after singing the praises of my skills, he offered me an apprenticeship program with his colleague who owned a home building company. I thanked him politely for the offer but explained to him that I had other plans. "What are your plans?" he asked. "I am going to be a race car driver," I told him. "A race car driver!" he snorted spontaneously; but he quickly regained his composure once he realised that I was serious, and he wished me luck with my future endeavours.

That was the very first time that I had ever told anyone, my parents included, that my goal was to become a race car driver. From that point on, I did everything that I could to make enough money to get to racing school. I am proud to say that although it took me a few more years than I had originally intended, to save the thousands of dollars to attend the Spenard David Racing School, I finally got there.

What a time that was for me... there I was, a young man in his mid-20s, who had finally made it to the threshold of his childhood dream. It was my time to show everyone at this school that I, Hugh Anderson, was going to be the next Mario Andretti!

The next three days included eating a great deal of humble pie, and lying in my hotel room at night with ice packs on my elbows and knees, questioning my chosen career. It was during these three days that I realized the importance of experience. While I had been trying to earn enough money to go to racing school, the sixteen-year-olds that I was up against this weekend, had been racing go-karts on their parents' dime since they were 6 or 7 years old, and had compiled many miles of track time. Although I did go to the racetrack on many more occasions, I quickly succumbed to my own three-strike rule. I was too big, too poor, and not crazy enough to make a living as a race car driver. Now, back to the drawing board, with that age old question: What am I going to do with my life?

The Day I Applied to Become a Licensed Driving Instructor

After the racing school debacle, I continued to look for different jobs—or more specifically, a career. I continued working at my high school job stocking grocery store shelves, and continued to help my friends with driving standards. Money earned went to buying a few different cars for me, all of which were standard.

One morning while looking at the local newspaper, I saw an ad for a licensed driving instructor. I thought, what the heck; I had been teaching friends and family members to drive standard on automobiles for years now. I applied for the job, but I was quickly informed that I didn't meet the criteria. The criterion was that the individual had to already be a licensed driving instructor. That conversation motivated me to research how to become a licensed driving instructor. I learned that in order to become licensed, one would have to attend a three-week-long course. It would also cost a great deal of money, with no guarantees at the end that you would even have a job. After a great deal of conversation with my family, I decided that I would find the money and attend the Ontario Safety League.

It was a bright Sunday morning with the sunshine streaming in as I completed the application to attend OSL, and dropped a cheque into the envelope. As I was leaving the house, I had just had words with my girlfriend (I don't recall what about), on the phone. I drove to the end of my street, to where the mailbox was located, dropped my application into the mail, and then continued to drive, allowing myself to cool down before returning home to call her back. Right now, you're probably asking yourself why the heck I am even telling you about this. I'm telling you this because I was about to learn another lesson or two.

While driving down a four-lane street near the local university, I was following two vehicles as the road began to curve to the right. I noticed three teenagers crossing the street. One had darted completely across the street, and the other two had crossed halfway, with their toes just edging onto the yellow line as we, in the three cars, were approaching. Being a typical young male myself, I simply glared at the two kids who were standing on the centre line, while unbeknownst to me, two vehicles in front, a woman had stopped her car and was getting out to yell at the other youth that had darted across the street in front of her. I noticed the brake lights on the vehicle in front; I hit the brakes and recognized that I couldn't go left because of the two youths standing on the line, and I couldn't make it to the right (momentum was pushing me left), so I slammed into the back of the vehicle in front of me. Was this an omen? I had never been in a car crash, and yet mere minutes after putting my driving instructor license application into the mail, I rear-ended someone?

Lessons learned here: Lesson #1 was that emotions can inhibit eye movement; in other words, don't drive angry! Lesson #2 was about following too close; and Lesson #3 was that collisions generally occur as a result of a combination of factors—in this case, kids jaywalking, my eyes being locked on what I perceived as the hazard, and the woman stopping and getting out of her car in a live lane of traffic. Remove any one of these three factors, and I wouldn't have crashed.

Emergency Vehicle Operation Instruction

Meeting My Supervisor Instructor

When I started at the Ontario Safety League to become a licensed driving instructor, we spent the first three days stuck inside a classroom. During the first three days, I had numerous opportunities to question my new career path. We spent a lot of time discussing the Highway Traffic Act, which covers the rules and regulations for the province of Ontario, and we were also introduced to the difference between andragogy and pedagogy teaching theories. Studying the science of how we learn, and delving deeper into psychology and sociology, really started to pique my interest. I was starting to appreciate teaching/instructing as opposed to just the hands-on driving skills. This little three-week program was starting to get interesting. Everyone in our class was looking forward to meeting their supervising driving instructor on the fourth day. Jerzy Kwiatkowski was introduced as my instructor, as well as that of two of my classmates. We had a quick meeting among the four of us to discuss our rendezvous point, and then we headed to our separate cars. As we got onto the highway and began following the instructor, the traffic was congested, and he was travelling very slowly. I felt it was unsafe, so I chose to pass him, and proceeded to meet the group at our rendezvous point. Even as I passed him, I was saying to myself, this isn't going to leave a very good impression with this gentleman. Once we all met up, he asked why I felt it was necessary to pass him. He listened to my rationale and praised my decision making, which led to a great discussion on the merits of safety vs compliance.

Unbeknownst to me at the time, this was the beginning of a long-term friendship. I will always remember one of his first pieces of feedback that he gave me: "Watching you parallel park was like watching a jetliner land." Although successful, it was very fast! LOL. This man taught me a great deal about time management, how to structure an in-vehicle lesson, and the overall business of being an independent driving instructor. Jerzy helped me get my first driving instructor job, as he introduced me to the owner of a driving school. A couple of years later, he lobbied the head of the Driving Instructors

Association into accepting me into the classroom instructor's training before I had completed the recommended prerequisite. He was also the one who submitted my name to the Ontario Police College/Academy to replace him when he vacated his position in 1998. Jerzy is just one of the many individuals who have helped me along my journey, and to whom I am extremely grateful.

Chapter 2

The Early Years of Training

"Tell me and I forget, teach me and I may remember, involve me and I learn."
– Benjamin Franklin

Dichotomy of Racing and Safe Driving

The first day that I began delivering in-car driving instruction, I remember driving up the street of my very first student, being very apprehensive. I wasn't concerned with my ability to teach this young man how to drive, but more importantly, I was asking myself: Am I a fraud?

Here I was, a young man who spent a great deal of his time driving very fast on city streets and country roads, and who loved going out on snowy days with intentions of getting his car as sideways as possible, and I was about to teach the next generation of drivers how to drive—or more specifically, to be safe! Thank goodness, I was following the basic driving instruction handbook, and I knew that I was going to be teaching the student the proper way to pass the road test and receive his driver's license. This conversation would continue inside my head as I drove, in between my students' pick-ups.

Once I began instructing the varied students, I started to really appreciate watching how the drivers were progressing. Some days, they would absolutely amaze me as to how far a driver could progress in as little time as 45 minutes. There was no doubt in my mind that I had found my calling; if only I could find a way to silence that little voice inside my head that was continually saying that I was a fraud. How did I overcome this, you might be thinking?

One day, the parents of one of my most difficult students asked me whether their son would be able to get his driver's license soon. They started questioning me about the driver examiner and what they would be looking for, and then they proceeded to tell me about all of the rumours that the teenagers were spreading amongst themselves; rumours such as, you always fail the first time you take the test; when you stop at stop signs, you have to count out loud to 3; and if you go over the speed limit by any amount for any moment of time, you will automatically fail. All of these points were absolutely false! What this conversation told me was that they weren't as concerned about their son driving safely; they were more worried about their son passing the test. In my mind, my job description wasn't to help kids pass a 10-minute road test, but it was to help foster a lifelong journey of safe driving. This conversation helped me quiet that little voice inside of my head, as I now recognized that I was teaching students the proper way to drive. If that meant they needed to be a few miles per hour over the speed limit in order to travel with the flow of traffic, so be it.

I've always told my students that it's one thing to be complying with the laws of the road, but it's another to be a danger to oneself while on the road. A quick analogy I often use is that someone who is driving well below the speed limit or, more importantly, the flow of traffic, can often be compared to the pebble or the rock in the middle of a river. As water approaches the rock, it becomes very turbulent as it is forced to move around the rock on both the left and the right. Much the same can be said about the person who is adamant about driving in their particular lane at or below the speed limit. A safe driver would find it more prudent to move into the slower lane and allow the traffic to pass by them in a much calmer manner.

One fact, which I'm very proud of, is that every single one of my students that went for their driver's license received it on the very first attempt. The reason being was twofold: First off, I was teaching them to be safe but also helping them understand why certain skills were being evaluated during a road test. For instance, a three-point turn is often misunderstood. This is the cornerstone of learning how the controls work on a vehicle, and the proper use of each. My homework to every one of my students was to practice a three-point turn at least 10 times before I saw them for the next session. This helped them all become very proficient at working the brakes, gas, gear selector, steering, etc. Secondly, I was always honest with my students. If I didn't feel that they were ready for the road test, I would encourage them to put it off until we agreed that they were ready.

How did I manage to balance racing and safe driving, you might ask? On a few occasions, I would actually take my students to a go-kart track, where we would spend a half-hour zipping around the track. It was with the hope of showing them that the place to play in a car and drive quickly is in a controlled environment, such as a go-kart track or even a racetrack. Not only was I the instructor who took the kids racing, but I was also the driving instructor who had a group of his students change a tire on his car just because they asked if they could do it.

It's very important to teach to the students' individual and distinct needs. If they are asking a question or have a concern, it's my intention to try to deal with it right then and there, because their mind is ready for the answer. I quickly learned that driver training has to be all about the student and not about the instructor.

Does Practice Make Perfect?

When I was hired on at the Skid Control School, which was Canada's longest running advanced driver training facility, I was required to practice a great deal before I went live with my first students. I have to admit that I found this very frustrating, because I believed that my abilities were ready for students. Doug Annett, owner of the school, sent me out onto the skin pad and told me to practice demonstrating the different maneuvers that were necessary for an advanced driving instructor. Once I felt I was ready to teach, I invited him out to the pad and had him assess my abilities.

Before I get to his assessment on the skid pad, I should probably go back to the very first day that I met him, during my job interview. Here, I sat with him as he and his business partner asked me questions in their office, with the interview lasting well over an hour. Just as I thought the interview was wrapping up, they asked me, "Are you ready to go for a drive in the car?" I have to admit that I was gobsmacked, because I was already exhausted and thinking about taking a nap. I guess, in reality, how could you be hiring a driving instructor if you haven't even seen them drive a car?

So, off we went to the streets for a drive; he guided me through his well-practiced route, providing very little feedback throughout. The drive lasted approximately 20 minutes, and I was very pleased with myself. Now it was feedback time, and he asked me about my very first lane change after we had departed the school. The shoulder check was admittedly very late as I was partially into the new lane before I had completed the check. I explained to him that I was pretty certain that it was clear. In fact, I went on to add that I was 99% certain that it was clear. I will never forget what he said to me next, without too much hesitation: "So, what you're telling me is that you are 99% certain it was clear. Then that would mean that for every 100 lane changes you make, there could be someone there." I have to admit, that one comment has resonated with me for my entire driving career, and I have utilized that line on many a student over the years.

Now let's get back to the skid pad evaluation. I knew that Doug had a very critical eye for driving and a very methodical approach to the driving task. I began my little commentary for the instructor demos, and everything was going well until I actually started the manoeuvre itself—I made a small mistake, and although I didn't spin totally around, it definitely wasn't smooth car control. Doug asked me to pull off the track, and he hopped out of the vehicle while saying for me to keep practicing the maneuvers. He even suggested that I be able to do it perfectly 10 times in a row in both directions. I can't tell you how many hundreds, if not thousands, of runs I made, but I was certain that on many occasions I would get 9 runs perfectly and then spin out on the 10th—once again, starting all over at the beginning

Some people would look back on those incidents and think, "Wow, what a hardass he must have been," but in reality, he was trying to push me to be the best that I could be, and for that I am grateful. I was never intimidated during any instructor demonstration because I knew that I was ready. In my mind, an advanced driving instructor must be able to perform the task perfectly when under the pressures of the students' watchful eyes. It's one thing to practice something, but it's another to practice perfectly in order to become perfect.

Invitation to the Police Academy

I had worked for the Ontario Safety League (OSL) as a Supervising Instructor, training new driving instructors for a short while. Unfortunately, I had to step away once I realized that business and training are often in conflict with each other. I had met with the president of the Safety League and explained to her that the calibre of drivers that had been taking the Driving Instructor course was very poor, and I was not willing to pass them as instructors because, in some cases, I questioned how they even got their driver's license in the first place. She was very diplomatic and explained to me that if we develop a reputation of having too high of a standard, then the students—or more importantly, the want-to-be driving instructors—would simply register with other places to get their instructor license. I understood where she was coming from and respectfully cut back on my hours with them, and focussed only on remedial training and specialized students.

One day when I was in the neighbourhood of the OSL, I stopped in for a quick hello, only to be invited into the president's office because she wanted to discuss something with me. While I sat at her desk, she made a phone call without really telling me who she was calling. I sat there and listened to her leave an extended voice message espousing the virtues of my training abilities, and she closed the message off with the line, "I really think that Hugh would be a benefit

Emergency Vehicle Operation Instruction

to the Ontario Police College (OPC) driving programs."

Two weeks later, I was being given a tour of OPC, and meeting numerous people, including the deputy director of the college, and I received a full tour of the Police Vehicle Operations building. At the end of the tour, I was asked if I could see myself working at the police college. They have seconded police officers training the new recruits, but they were lacking professional driving instruction abilities and/or techniques. Of course, I said yes—I would have open access to a driver training track, skid pad, and hundreds of drivers—how could I say no? This was going to be so much fun because I would finally be able to get back to where my heart was, which is advanced driving skills on a track—*high performance driving*. Finally, I was able to be where I wanted to be.

Truth be known, this is where my eyes were opened to the fact that most collisions involving law enforcement officers are not emergency related. Most collisions occur while on patrol or normal destination driving, where no emergency response is required. I had an opportunity to sit down and go through thousands—yes, I said thousands—of collision reports involving police officers in a Metropolitan Police Service. It amazed me as to how many collisions were of the basic *we rear-end somebody, they rear-end us, we turn not in safety, they turn not in safety, we back into poles, the poles jump in front of us,* etc.

Just basic motor vehicle collisions or, as some people would say, accidents. I don't believe in these being accidents, but I will leave that discussion for later in the book.

The Need to Prove Oneself

Ego: *Your ego is your conscious mind, the part of your identity that you consider your "self." If you say someone has "a big ego," then you are saying he is too full of himself.*

I really struggled with where exactly to put this section in this book. It was really a combination of my training at the Skid Control School and at the Ontario Police College, where I recognised that ego could be detrimental to training.

Working at the Skid Control School, my students were primarily professional drivers but not in the same vein that you would think. These are people who spend a great deal of time behind the wheel of an automobile. These could be sales representatives, engineers, technicians, delivery personnel, etc. On average, this group would be driving anywhere from 25,000 to 60,000 miles per year.

They all drove a significant amount of time, but they never really focused on the art of driving or how to be safer drivers, because they never thought of driving as part of their job. That's where our (SCS) job was to help them recognize the importance of driving safely, both for the company's bottom line and, more importantly, for their own well-being.

I often thought it was my job to demonstrate, at a high level, my ability to control a vehicle, whether it is on the skid pad or driving on the city streets, as we demonstrated appropriate defensive driving strategies.

When I went to the police college, I also felt the same pressure every time I took the wheel of the car. I knew that the students were watching me with the hopes of me making a mistake, and I would often feel the need to show them just how good I was.

Once I had completed my first recruit class at the OPC, I returned to the Skid Control School to work for them between recruit classes. The owners of the school met with me before I returned to OPC for my second recruit class, and they made mention of how my skills seemed to have evolved as an instructor while being away at the OPC. What I had now begun to understand was that I didn't need to prove myself to either the students at OPC or the clients at the SCS, because I had the knowledge, skills, and ability to help each and every one of them become a better driver and, ultimately, to be the best that they can be.

Not very often does anyone get to see me drive (track) at full speed anymore. Proving that I am better or how good I am is not part of my job description. This is something that we work very hard on with our field training officers these days. Yes, we do need the FTO to model the appropriate driving behaviours, but on the other hand, we also have to allow the rookie the opportunity to develop their police driving skills under the FTO's tutelage.

I know that we face an uphill challenge here because this is something that took me a couple of years to come to terms with, but perhaps it just came with maturity.

Why Can't They Drive?

The Ontario Police College is our provincial academy, where every police officer goes for the basic constable training. I quickly realized that although driving is one of the most dangerous tasks that police officers face, it is not held in the same regard as Defensive Tactics or Firearms training.

This really shouldn't surprise me, given that the general society in North America feels the same way about driving. If someone has an accident, then that is what it was, and it is just a fact of life. In my reality, this is not the case; most collisions could be prevented if one or more of the drivers involved did just one thing differently.

The recruits at the college would be exposed to many different driving exercises, both on a closed course at the OPC track, as well as on the country roads and streets around the neighboring town, which has a population of around 7,500.

The program would often start with the recruits being on the skid pad, to not only help them with skid correction but, more importantly, to get a better feel for the car. From there, they would go to the little town for a drive, taking a look at the basic driving skills and their understanding of the rules of the road. Both of these areas, I had a great deal of experience with, and I relished the opportunity to meet the different personalities that would get behind the wheel of my car. What surprised me most, perhaps, was hearing the background story of each of these individuals, and recognizing just how varied they were. The one thing that stood out to me was just how different they were compared to me when it came to driving. Most of these individuals had spent a great deal of their teenage years studying for college and university, and most likely relied on public transit as opposed to having their own car. This often became apparent both on the skid pad—where some recruits were afraid that the vehicle was going to roll over—and with their nervousness dealing with traffic in the little town near the college.

I couldn't get over the fact that people couldn't reverse into a parking spot at the local coffee shop, or that they were unable to look far enough down the road to see stopped motorists, and of course, their inability to recognize one-way traffic signs. Wow, was this ever disappointing to me. This dashed my hopes that working at the OPC would allow me to help the recruits advance and become proficient high-performance drivers out on the track. It now became very clear to me that I wasn't necessarily going to make high-performance drivers out of them, and that I was simply going to help them become better basic drivers. The 45-year-old sales reps that I used to train would be able to drive circles around these recruits.

Herein lies the problem: For the past few years, prior to beginning work at the OPC, I had been training experienced drivers. In fact, I would say that they were professional drivers due to the amount of mileage they drove every year. Unfortunately for the recruit class that I first faced at OPC, this is who I was comparing them to. Needless to say, the recruits that I trained were often invited back for a driving workshop after regular hours. My fellow trainers nicknamed me "the Hammer." This was a little euphemism for me crushing their spirits. Interestingly enough, these workshops allowed the trainers—me included—to spend more one-on-one time with the students, which ultimately led to them becoming much more proficient behind the wheel.

Fun with Cone Courses

Cone courses, or sometimes known as pylon courses, are often the foundation of many EVOC training programs. I have to admit that one of the true pleasures I get while training EVOC programs is designing the track layout and practicing it until it becomes finalized.

In saying that, may I suggest that you always design a new layout, by yourself or perhaps with one other person. I learned this valuable lesson one day while having eight other people around as I was trying to lay out a brand new cone exercise on a skid pad. While the others were trying out the course and helping me come up with the appropriate spacing, I managed to frustrate almost half of the drivers. No matter how many times I said that I didn't have the track layout correct yet, it didn't seem to resonate with them at all. It took a great deal of practice and patience to get those eight off of the ledge. It would have been so much easier had I just quietly worked by myself on that one afternoon, and then once I believed it was ready, have them come and give it a try.

I highly recommend that whenever designing a cone course, you always start off with an existing one and build from there. If you think it's easy, I suggest you pull out a blank piece of paper, start designing a course, and then transfer that course from paper to the track and/or parking lot.

Prior to beginning a new track layout, you must ask yourself a couple of questions: What do I want the driver to get out of the exercise? What do I want the instructors/evaluator to get out of the exercise?

This is one of the fundamentals of being a good course designer/instructor. Often, what an instructor sees from outside the vehicle is much different than the average person. Are you evaluating eye placement or improper vehicle positioning? Or perhaps you're looking for the student to discover the difference of having a balanced or unbalanced platform.

Over the years, my training philosophy on cone courses has changed. Early on, I wanted to create some sort of stress or pressure, and have the driver push themselves and challenge themselves against the stopwatch. I've come to realize that using the stopwatch can be a very dangerous tool when it comes to the driver psyche, especially if you add in competition with their peers!

I now will use either the stopwatch or competition, but never both at the same time. If we can make training fun for the students, and be able to engage with them, they most certainly will get more out of it. That's where I will use the competition side of training but always keep it light, ensuring that the students are supportive of each other. When I use the stopwatch to try and get someone to improve their performance, it will only be at the end of the training; it's then our opportunity to see if they're able to keep the same skills up while working under the pressure of the stopwatch. Ultimately, you want them to be the best that they can be. Perhaps we should put the caveat out there that not all students will react in the same way to the pressure of their peers watching, or to the pressure of the stopwatch ticking.

    Considering that we are training our students to be on the streets in live traffic, where the demands of being perfect are imperative, we should not allow them to get careless or dangerous while driving on a cone course. My philosophy is this: There are no time penalties in the real world; therefore, we shouldn't apply time penalties at the track. If you touch a cone and it wobbles, you haven't made it to the call.

Chapter 3

Mistakes That I've Made

*"Live as if you were to die tomorrow.
Learn as if you were to live forever."*
– Mahatma Gandhi

Failing to Respect Learning Styles

Soon after I began working for a large municipal police service, my training partner of just over a year, received an invitation to instruct at the Ontario Police College (OPC), on a two-year secondment. This was great news for him but not for me, because I would have to break in a new partner. Our boss gave us two days to train the new instructor to be my partner.

I decided that we would treat him just like a student/recruit officer, so we asked him to play the role of the student, and that way he would see how my partner and I interacted and ultimately trained our recruits.

Sounds simple, right? WRONG! There were many factors that I didn't take into account. My new partner had been an officer for well over 20 years, and he had some expectations and couldn't stop that little voice inside his head from thinking that we were trying to catch him making mistakes behind the wheel, to make him appear incompetent. Let me just say that this day was a disaster. From a quick little outburst from him, stating that he wasn't up for these games, to him going home early, I definitely hadn't started our new partnership off on the right foot.

That night, I had an opportunity to reflect on the day—just how bad it was and how I made things so uncomfortable for all three of us. It would be easy for me to say that it was his fault and that he was unable to go with the flow, and I know that many people would have done just that, but something wasn't sitting right with me. When I first arrived at the office the next day, I put the entire outline of the day on the board, including what our goal was and when we would be having breaks, including lunch. The student outcomes were also clearly outlined for the three scenarios that we were about to perform.

To say that this day was a success would be a total understatement. He was a great student. He did exactly as he was asked, and the three of us got along extremely well.

Although I may prefer to react to situations and go with the flow and be very informal, I have come to realize that some do not perform well in that arena. In fact, some people, just like my new partner, find that way of training very unsettling and are unable to meet the challenges presented to them. More often than not, people need to know what the expectations are and what the process will look like. These two days were probably the most important lessons learned when it comes to *training the trainer*.

What Do You Mean, "It's Not About Me?"

As an EVO instructor, it's obvious that we like to drive vehicles. One of the toughest challenges for those of us involved in policing is to allow others, aka the students, to do the majority of the driving. When the opportunity arises, we love to give demonstrations. Here's an example, where it's clearly obvious that this wasn't as much a demonstration as it was to show how good we instructors are. It was a beautiful sunny day at the police college, and I was one of three instructors training a group of nine recruit constables. Today's exercise was to deliver Rolling Block training: three fully marked cruisers blocking in one suspect vehicle. We were conducting the training on a paved access road (driveway) that was about half a mile long but not particularly straight; therefore, we always kept speeds below 60 km (40 mph). The training had gone well, with all nine students demonstrating a good understanding of the technique, and able to meet our standard. Looking at his watch, one of our instructors said that we had enough time for one more run, so he suggested that we (indicating the three instructors) do a demonstration on just how this should really be done. Full disclosure: I was 100% on board with this plan at the time. I was driving the suspect vehicle, he was driving the lead vehicle, and our third instructor was taking up the second position—unfortunately, we needed one of the students to take up the final position at the rear.

So off I go, accelerating up to speed. "Heck, it's the instructor," I say to myself. "We can go faster." I was probably doing 80 km an hour as I hit the first curve, and the other two cars accelerated past me at well over a hundred kilometres an hour as they moved into position. Everything was going well until I looked in my mirror and saw the final vehicle swerving off the road at well over 100 kilometres an hour, and all I kept saying to myself was, "Don't hit the trees, don't hit the trees, don't hit the trees…"

I am very thankful to report that he did not hit any trees, but I'm sure the three lads that were in that vehicle had a rude awakening as they were spinning out into the field. We were 3 professional Police Vehicle Operations instructors, trying to show these young recruits how it should be done. What an error in judgment on our behalf. In fact, as I look back on my entire career, I can honestly say that any time one of my students lost control, hit something, etc., I could always blame myself for not recognizing that I was putting them in a position well beyond their skill set.

Instructor Showboating

One of the exercises that we used to train officers who had already returned from OPC (Academy), was a slow speed vehicle maneuvering exercise. For this exercise, there would be myself and my partner instructing three to four new officers. The goal of this exercise was to help them become more comfortable with a large vehicle (Crown Victoria), and it included a great deal of reversing. In order to do that, we needed to work on vision skills and vehicle placement in order to ensure that we had the proper space to manoeuvre the vehicle.

This was an opportunity to show the young officers just how proficient a driver could be with the Crown Vic. In other words, professionalism should come to mind. More often than not, I would demonstrate this exercise with all three students inside the car with me. Occasionally, my partner would demonstrate the exercise. My partner, at this time, wasn't crazy about doing the demonstration, but he would begrudgingly look after it if I had another task to take care of at the time. One day, I noted that if he clipped a cone, he would then over accelerate, causing the rear of the vehicle to fishtail and generally hit three to four more cones. The students would exit the vehicle laughing, having enjoyed their ride, and I would simply chalk this up to him showboating once again. If the instructors drove the car like that, it gave permission to the students to do the very same thing. On about the third or fourth time watching my partner do the exact same thing, it suddenly dawned on me: Him driving like this was simply masking his inability to do the exercises cleanly/properly. With some empathy and compassion, I explained my observations to him, and I asked if he would be open to having me train him on the exercise. I am pleased to say that he was open to that training session, and from that day forward, he relished the opportunity to conduct the demonstration drive with the students—and I don't believe I ever saw him strike a cone again.

Speaking of instructor demonstrations, I noted a certain phenomenon earlier in my career: If an instructor demonstration isn't as perfect as it could be, it would lead to a poor performance by the students. More often than not, if I hit a cone or made a mistake in my demonstration, it would come back to haunt me, as the students themselves would struggle to complete a clean run.

Much like I stated earlier, only perfect practice makes perfect, and I will explain the importance of this in greater detail later on, when we discuss the four stages of competency.

Slowing Things Down, Speeds Learning Up (Scaffolding)

There are many different interpretations of scaffolding theories when it comes to teaching and learning, and I don't want to get into that debate today. For this chapter, and to keep it very simple, I am using the term "scaffolding," meaning to build upon previously learned skills.

In some training programs, instructors often fail to start off with the basics, and they move right into performance driving and/or emergency response. In my mind, there's no sense in teaching a new officer how to go against/take a red light, if they don't know where to stop for a red light in the first place when driving in their personal vehicle.

I don't know about you, but I can tell a great deal about a driver's skills just by watching them approach a red light, or even an all-way stop sign. Where do they look? Are they checking the mirror to see what's happening behind? Are they glancing right, looking for pedestrians, joggers, or roller bladders? Do they look to the left to see any traffic approaching? Perhaps most important in this case, where do they actually stop? Once the light turns green, where do they look? Do they even look left/right, or do they just accelerate through? These are all things that I would like to know about someone's driving habits prior to asking them to drive in an emergency response or to go against a red light.

Before a new officer begins an emergency response drive, it's imperative that they know where to look. Where are the hazards coming from, and how can they predict potential conflict? More importantly, how can they minimize or mitigate conflict? Take the time to clean up your students' basic driving before you start putting them into a heightened emotional state. We will expand further on this when we discuss tunnel vision, with the four stages of competence, later on in the book.

I realize that all of our students will arrive to us as a fully licensed driver—well, most of the time they will. When they arrive, they have high expectations of the training that they are about to receive and believe themselves to be above-average drivers. Having an opportunity to go out into a vehicle with your students, allows you to see how they drive along as if they were going to the neighborhood grocery store. It allows you an opportunity to see how they position their vehicle in and amongst other traffic, where they look as they are driving, and perhaps more importantly, where they look while turning corners.

Most of you may not have an opportunity to take your students into live traffic, so I would suggest that when you introduce them to your track, or even a cone course for that matter, you start off at a very basic level.

When I say basic level, I mean keeping speeds lower to allow the student the opportunity to understand the layout of the course and/or track, but along the way, there should be some artificial stop signs built into the course.

When I was working at the police college, I had a student who had emigrated from the United Kingdom, where he was a police officer already. We had just met as he hopped into my car, and we were headed out onto the track to do some cornering exercises at a moderately high speed. I had never been in a car with him before and I knew that he had missed the previous track (introduction) session but the one thing that stood out in my mind was he had already been a police officer so therefore we shouldn't have any problems.

The exercise that I had him engage in almost immediately once we hit the track was called; follow me – just another name for follow the leader. Another instructor was driving a lead vehicle and two to three students would be following in their marked vehicles. At the same time there were at least one and sometimes two other teams doing the exact same exercise on the track. By design we were meant to cross each other's paths and interact with each other but of course we should gradually build up to this level as the student would build their confidence prior to engaging with one of the other groups of cars. Unfortunately I had assumed (and we know what happens when you assume) that my driver was ready to interact with other trafficked immediately. This proved to be a significant error on my part - not my students, but mine! As we came around the corner my driver had carried a little too much speed and was already encroaching on the Center line when he noticed the oncoming cars. He reacted; but unfortunately, he reacted to his previously learned (habit) skill and swerved to the left where the oncoming vehicle was already starting to swerve moving right. Let me tell you, there was no paint exchanged between vehicles, but I may have dropped a few "maple buds" in my jockey shorts, LOL. Yes, easy to laugh at now, but at the time, what a catastrophic error I had made.

I failed to scaffold him properly. We should've reviewed the previous training and perhaps used another driver to be the first participant in my car. This would have allowed my driver an opportunity to get used to the track, remind him of proper eye placement on corners, and help build his confidence so that when he did take the wheel and ultimately encounter a potential hazard, he would have been more prepared to deal with it. It's my understanding that this was the only time, in the many hours of PVO training he attended, that he reverted back to his United Kingdom habits of driving on the wrong side of the road!

Relaxing in the Front Seat (Never Wear Red)

Way back in the first couple of years of teaching new drivers, I had an opportunity to train one of the most challenging students of my career. At the time, I had no idea just how much she would teach me about being a good instructor.

I received a call from the owner of my driving school and was asked if I would be interested in training a woman who was in her late

30s and had recently immigrated to Canada to raise her children. When I began training her, I realized that communication wasn't a problem, because she was very proficient at the English language and was highly educated; however, she had absolutely no hand-eye coordination and had never been behind the wheel of an automobile in her past.

Yes, we spent a great deal of time discussing what the two pedals on the floor were for, and I must say that I was very thankful that we weren't learning what the clutch pedal was for, as we were in an automatic, LOL.

This driver required many, many hours of driver instruction because she didn't have anyone to practice with in order for her to garner experience. We spent many a session in the same neighbourhood, one which didn't have any curbs and little traffic. One day, we were practicing both right hand turns and left hand turns, and just going around the block. She was finally starting to get the hang of it. She was looking up the road as she was accelerating smoothly out from the corner, allowing the steering wheel to slide back through her fingertips. Finally, I could start to relax in the right-hand seat. I decided to take out my clipboard and jot down a few notes in preparing for her next session, when I felt a slight bump—I looked up to see that we had now driven off of the paved roadway and down into the smallest of culverts on someone's front lawn. Directly in our path was an elderly man dressed in red from head to toe, raking his leaves. I managed to reach over to the wheel and turn the car left; we continued back through the little culvert and up onto the paved road, and continued on our merry way. I have to be honest with you; I did drive by much later, after dropping my student off, and I could clearly see the tire marks on the grass. That phrase that is commonly used during EVO instruction—"people steer where they look"—was never so true, and left an indelible mark on my brain.

I'm sure that if you have any amount of experience as a driver trainer, you know that sitting in the right front seat is way more stressful than sitting in the driver's seat. This is never truer than when you have a very inexperienced driver or when it is raining out. I can't tell you how many days I went home with a splitting headache just because it was raining. Straining to see further up the road, trying to give timely information to the driver, and tensing up every time they accelerated out of a corner, all led to an evening with Tylenol. Truth be known, no one was happier than me, knowing that traction control and/ or ESP was engaged on one of our training vehicles.

Chapter 4

Lessons Learned

"In learning you will teach, and in teaching you will learn."
– Phil Collins

The Importance of a Plan

Early in my driving instruction career, when I was studying to become a Classroom Driving Instructor, I submitted 3 or 4 lesson plans to the master instructor for evaluation. I decided that there was no way that he was going to read every single lesson plan, considering there were over 30 people in our class. So I wrote an extra line into one of my learning outcomes: "John, do you really read all of this B.S.?" You can imagine my surprise when I received my lesson plans back and I read his comments, written in red ink on the front of my lesson plans, saying, "Thank you for making me laugh so hard that I actually woke my wife at 1 a.m.!"

Early in my driver instruction career, I recognized the importance of having a good plan, outlining what is expected of the student, and what the objective is. Additionally, I recognized the importance of letting the student in on the objective and understanding the process. This really helps the student clear their headspace, and allows them to perform the tasks at hand without continually worrying or questioning why they are doing something, or what the instructor is thinking, etc.

Emergency Vehicle Operation Instruction

In the previous chapter, I mentioned how poorly my day went when trying to train my new partner, having not given him a clear understanding of what our objectives were or how we were going to get there. The same can be said when working as a team of instructors. You may have an idea of what the objective is and how you're going to get there, but if you don't share that with the rest of your team, then that can lead to a very frustrating day, not only for you and your teammates but for your students as well.

I was very fortunate to have worked with a few partners who could quite easily adapt to an ever- changing agenda. One of my favourite partners would often joke that "working with Hugh is like reaching into a box of Bits and Bites, where every day is a whole new ballgame." I look back on that now and realize how frustrating that must have been for my partners. On the other hand, some relished the opportunity to work with me, and quickly began to understand that my thought process was always on getting the student to progress by challenging them to adapt to the different situations that presented themselves.

Some learners are just fine with receiving verbal instructions and/or an overview of the day, while others would like to read it—in their minds, they comprehend information differently. I also like to read the instructions myself, because I feel it allows me to process information at my speed.

As an instructor, we are always feeling the time crunch, and it seems that we never have enough time to deliver the training, which we know is so beneficial to our students. One of the ways that we can manage our students' preferred comprehension methods is to have the outline or objective up on the whiteboard, or perhaps on the video screen, before the class even arrives to the room. You don't even have to read it to them; simply having it up on the board allows them to read it as they're waiting for the class or session to begin. If you have a history with these students, and they know that this is your practice, they will easily fall into the habit of reading it before the class begins. It will also open the door for a well-thought-out question, as opposed to a student asking something just for the sake of asking.

Training for the Student, Not the Instructor

> *"When you are the first to **laugh** at yourself, everyone laughs **with** you...not **at** you."*
> – Unknown

I've noticed that humour, fun, and laughter are all good tools and indicators when it comes to training. I've come to appreciate some good old-fashioned pranks, especially in policing. I've also witnessed some not so useful applications of humour. I have worked with people over the years, not specifically in driver training but also in Use-of-Force and Academic, where I sometimes wonder why they are doing what they are doing. It would appear that some instructors are just going through the motions to get to the end of the day and go home. I have also worked with the total opposite, where people have a true passion for training and want to ensure that they give their students everything they can to help ensure a long and safe career.

I hate to admit that I also have been guilty of doing something in order to make fun of the student—just because I was bored. Yes, at the time, I could articulate that I was trying to make a point, but in reality, it wasn't necessary to do that. Example number 1: In live traffic, I was leading a Follow Me exercise, and the driver was struggling with keeping sight of my vehicle, not that I was travelling too fast, but she was unable to identify vehicles, and she kept getting confused. I made it my goal to position my vehicle in behind her without her seeing me. Her classmates thought it was great fun; however, she did not. I don't think she learned a great deal during that session. On another occasion, however, I can say that our student adopted the philosophy of the quote at the beginning of this chapter. Code name Starbucks: It was the same exercise, called Follow Me, but on this occasion, we had a driver who was performing at a much higher level, and therefore we decided to challenge him with a few more U-turns and changes of direction. He was supposed to spot me going in the opposing direction, radio to me that he had the vehicle in sight, and keep on transmitting his location, speeds, road conditions, etc.

At one point in time, I lost sight of him in my rear-view mirror, and yet he had been coming up the road that I was on, and in my direction of travel. I did a U-turn and went back down to my original street, where once again, he updated my location and direction of travel; however, I still had no sight of him... "Okay, one more U-turn and I'll find out what is going on, and why I can't see him," I kept saying to myself. Once again, I heard my student transmit that I was now going northbound, and he gave my location... I could now overhear my partner in the background yelling to him, "Tell him, tell him!" The driver then transmitted, "Dispatch, the vehicle is now northbound, and I am unable to follow because I am stuck in the Starbucks drive-thru." You see, he chose to cut through a parking lot to get around traffic, and he inadvertently ended up in a Starbucks drive-thru, with no means of escape.

We were very fortunate that our driver knew that our goal wasn't to make fun of him, but that we were simply challenging him with driving that had more of an assertive nature. He had a good laugh over this, and we, of course, laughed right along with him. I still smile every time I see him today, thinking back to that auspicious day when I nicknamed him Starbuck.

One final thought: Many years ago, I saw an interview with a Walt Disney executive, where he stated something to the effect that an employee at Disney World would never be criticized for a decision they make, if it was made with the intention of enhancing their guests' experience. That statement has stuck with me and is the philosophy from which I try my best to apply to our training programs. After all, it should always be about the guest/student.

Bridging the Track to the Road

Having spent countless hours of training on a skid pad, I feel that it's necessary to point out one of the flaws with training in a sterile/closed environment.

As an EVO instructor, we spend a great deal of time and energy trying to get our students to look well down the road toward their intended path. I like to try and get them to look off to the horizon, and ideally there is something on the horizon they can look at (i.e. a tree, a light pole, perhaps a vehicle parked off in the distance). By getting them a target to look at, they will be less apt to look down at the cones lying on the track. We all know that if we can get our drivers to do this, they will be much more successful in controlling the skidding vehicle. We also know that the majority of our students will have enjoyed the challenge of controlling the vehicle on the skid pad, and most likely will have had a great day. Any training we deliver on a skid pad always evokes a 10 on the feedback or course evaluation.

What happens next? The student hops into their personal vehicle at the end of the day, and away they go, having forgotten everything they just learned. In their eyes, they don't see the correlation between a skidding car on a skid pad and a vehicle on the city streets. They can't practice skid control while they drive home, or can they? Yeah, yeah, I know; all of you are laughing, having just envisioned them trying to skid around every corner and turn. Realistically speaking, it's imperative that we take whatever skills they worked on, whether being on a skid pad or out on a cone course, and have them apply it to their everyday driving.

Sometimes I'll get into the definition of a skid and what happens every time we turn a corner—the back tires have to slip across the pavement as they lose grip, in order for them to follow the front part of the vehicle. If you understand that concept, you should also understand that every time you turn the corner, you are actually fixing a skid. We can get the driver to look well down the road, and they will automatically have their eyes in the correct spot should the vehicle ever start to oversteer.

At the end of every track session, we, the EVO instructors, should remind our students how to practice out on the road, whether it means to look at the second set of traffic lights as they turn a corner, or whether it means that they look at the tree line in the distance, and allow their peripheral vision to help them complete the corner, centered in their lane.

There's one cone course that I have used on many occasions, and a key component to it is a tight little box where we have the student conduct a U-turn. It's imperative to have the student reduce their speed and take advantage of all the available space. If they do not, they quickly learn that a vehicle turning like this tends to be pushed out and wider, and will not be able to conduct the U-turn within the confines of the cones. This is a great exercise to get them to straight line brake, get their eyes out the side window, and have their hands follow their eyes as they smoothly accelerate out of the turn. By the end of the session, the student will be quite proficient with completing a U-turn.

I am very fortunate that I often have an opportunity to see the student again, either the next day or the next week, when we are out on city streets and in live traffic. It never surprises me that when I ask the student to conduct a U-turn for the first time of the day, they are unable to complete it within the confines of the roadway, and they feel that they need to climb the curb to complete it. This is now a great opportunity to apply the lessons we learned in earlier sessions out on the track, and to remind the student to do the same thing here on the road. More often than not, this is the last error they make while completing a U-turn with me. Over the years now, I've come to learn that once we complete the track training, I should give the students some suggestions for them to practice on their own when driving their personal vehicle.

Patience Is Key

When I first started as a driving instructor, I didn't realize just how frustrating it could be, sitting in the right front seat, watching people make bad decisions. Once I changed my mindset and realised that it was my job to help them improve their decision-making process, and not to make the decisions for them, I settled into a better place conceptually.

Ultimately, it came down to patience. Once I understood that I was getting paid to sit in the right front seat, and to help my students become the best drivers that they can be, the job became easy. No matter how many times we went around the same block or I had to remind them to look further down the road, it didn't matter, because I was getting paid.

If you start to yell—or as I like to say, "bark at the students,"—you will find that they may actually start to perform at a lower level and make even more mistakes because the stress hormones are starting to kick in. When this happens, the brain stops processing information as quickly; in fact, your driver may actually start to develop *tunnel vision*. You may try and argue that policing is about stress, and the officer needs to learn how to work under pressure; however, this isn't necessarily the place to put them under said pressure. We'll talk more about that, later in the book, when we get to the four stages of competence.

I have had numerous people, probably close to hundreds, say that I have "the patience of Job"—whatever that means. That is one thing I learned from being a driving instructor, but I also have truly improved as my stepchildren have taught me a great deal about the importance of patience. That, however, is for another book…

The Importance of Non-EVO Training

As I stated in the book, when I first got into police driver training, I believed that it was going to involve a lot of high speed driving on a track. I quickly learned, however, that many new recruits are not ready for this type of driving because their personal driving was still at a substandard level.

If you look at the collision statistics for not only law enforcement but for fire & EMS as well, you will note that the majority of incidences do not involve lights and sirens. In fact, the policing collisions will most likely be while they are on general patrol. What are we doing about this? Is the academy driver training program doing enough to ensure that the basic driving is at a high enough level, and are they ready to progress toward advanced driving principles. Let's be honest here; the same principles for advanced driving are at play in basic driving.

If a driver doesn't know where to look when they are driving down a city street approaching an intersection, then how would you expect them to know where to look when travelling down the same street but at a much higher speed? I feel sorry for all those brand new officers who have no post- academy driver training, because they have been put into a position of risk, having not been trained appropriately. The old saying that "if they have a driver's license, they should be good to go," must be put to rest, ASAP!

Later on in the book, we will discuss *commentary driving*, and we will expand on where drivers should be looking as they approach intersections or any potential hazards. One of the biggest risks I see facing young officers today without training, are with those whose normal habits are to drive less than 1 second off the bumper of the vehicle in front of them. They might be able to get away with that when they are driving their own car to the grocery store, but they will not be able to get away with that when they are being distracted. An emergency vehicle is laden with distractions, such as the computer, listening to the radio, and of course, looking for either an address or a suspect—all of which certainly sound like distracted driving to me.

Chapter 5

Cone Courses and Track Training

"Competition gives me energy. It keeps me focussed."
— Connor McGregor

Seating Fundamentals

Finally, I've gotten to the point of track training and/or cone course training. I have to admit that this is where I have the most fun in being an EVO instructor. This is an opportunity to put students into an environment that most of them have never had the opportunity to be in.

This is where proper seating position comes into place. I know that when all drivers got their original driver's license and/or learner's permit, they were taught how to adjust the seat and mirrors, etc. We know that most of them have been shown incorrectly, and that this will become very evident once we begin the track training. I often think of my first time that I was in a real race car on an actual track. I was in a mid-80s IROC Camaro, with a five-point harness, full roll cage, etc. I adjusted my seat and had someone buckle me in prior to heading out onto the track. We were in a line of five vehicles, with an instructor leading the pack in a road car. On the first lap, everything felt good; I was very excited to be in the race car, learning the proper racing lines on a track. The grin on my face must have been bursting out of my helmet, because I finally had the opportunity to show these instructors just what I could do. It turned out that I couldn't do much, because by the time I was finishing lap number two, I realized that I couldn't work the steering wheel properly, as I could no longer reach it due to the forces pushing me back into the seat. So, into the pits I pulled. Talk about first impressions being lasting impressions... That was a massive fail!

I'm very quick to point out this little story to many of my students as I'm helping them learn the appropriate sitting position. I'm always trying to remind them that the steering wheel isn't something to hang on to but is simply there to guide the vehicle along its path. I use the term "guide" specifically, because I can recall when I was first introduced to track training, and how the instructors barely had three fingers on the steering wheel, but I was hanging on for dear life as a passenger, as we hurtled around the track.

Here is where I will always dispel the myth about seat belts, starting off with reminding them that the seat belt is the most significant vehicle safety enhancement that has ever been developed in the motor vehicle industry—it saves lives! The seatbelt is what keeps the driver in the tactical position of being behind the steering wheel. If the seat belt is doing its job, the driver can concentrate on guiding the car, as opposed to hanging onto the car.

Conversely, if we allow our students to grip the steering wheel too tightly, they're causing a lot of tension in their arms, shoulders, and all the way up to their neck muscles. It's far more difficult to move our entire arms rather than just gently guide with fingers, wrists, and forearms.

I find that most drivers tend to sit too far back from the steering wheel, just like I did on my first-ever track experience, but on the rare occasion, I will encounter someone who's trying to eat the steering wheel, because they are way too close, but those are few and far between.

I will often start the seating procedure from the foot up. The left foot on the dead pedal for the foot plant, with the right foot being able to pivot between the throttle and the brakes. From there, we move on up to the arms. There are a couple of ways I can ensure that they are sitting an appropriate distance from the steering wheel. Ideally, I would like a 90-degree bend at the elbow, and then, after that, I will sometimes have them place their wrist over the top of the steering wheel, up at the 12 o'clock position. If their wrist bends after the steering wheel, they are generally in the appropriate seating position.

Student Engagement

I have walked into many a classroom and felt coolness within the room, as the students are generally disinterested in being in training, or more specifically, inside the confines of a classroom. Ice-breakers come in very handy at this point in time, but if I have my druthers with any driver training program I am delivering, whether it is police, EMS, or private individuals, my preference would always be to get them on a track or cone course before I take them out onto the city streets. Why is that? I hope you're asking. I do that because they are generally excited about being put into a new environment, and we've taken them outside of their comfort zone. In other words, this means they will open up their minds to what the instructors have to tell them. Having students behind the wheel on a cone course or track will often lead to smiles. As I mentioned earlier in the book, if the student is enjoying themselves, and smiling and laughing, they will be much more receptive to what you're saying, and more often than not will walk away having improved their driving skills.

Even on a simple course of cones, I will do my best to try and get them driving as soon as possible. Some courses may have too many cones and will be overwhelming to many a driver. If that is the case, try and break the course down into smaller segments to get them driving sooner. Once they've demonstrated an understanding of the course, or proficiency of said skill, then you can go ahead and introduce the entire layout to them.

I've mentioned throughout this book that it's very important that you have a plan and understand what skills you are trying to improve upon within your students. Be honest; sometimes it's not a skill—sometimes it's just to get them to open up to listening to what the instructors have to say. In other words, it's one big ice-breaker!

Time vs Accuracy

One of the things that never ceases to amaze me within the different EVO programs throughout North America is the inconsistencies on what standards we should be training to. I have either attended or audited numerous track exercises from all across North America. At some agencies, they're using the stopwatch and a clipboard to keep track of how many cones get struck or how many get knocked down; while at other schools, you are not permitted to strike a single cone.

Earlier in the book, I mentioned working with a partner who had difficulty in demonstrating what I like to call "a clean run," without striking a single cone. If you are hitting cones during demos, then you are saying that it's okay for your students to do likewise. Also, when we use the stopwatch and tally the number of cone strikes, it doesn't equate to teaching professionalism. Wouldn't it be more appropriate to train drivers to be successful and to be able to get to their calls, without having mayhem in the rear-view mirror? Of course, it would be! If that's the case, then why not teach the appropriate skills (i.e. proper eye placement) well ahead of your intended path, positioning the vehicle to take advantage of the available space, and to understand the importance of a balanced platform as you transition from one driver input to another.

One of the foundations of any track training that I like to build upon is always being in control and driving within one's skill level. Yes, the track and/or cone course is a good place to discover that level, but once you realize that you are beyond your skillset, then what? As you're beginning to practice, I would suggest applying the 80% rule, or driving at 8/10s. In other words, always leave a little bit in your back pocket so that if you do make a mistake, there is still some room for recovery if you've gone a little too fast into your corner, or left your braking too late, etc. If, however, you have been driving at 10/10s and something goes wrong, there is no margin for error, and you're definitely going to end up in a whole lot of hurt! As instructors, we should try to instill this mindset in our officers, especially as they are taking the skills on the road with them.

Some students that I have worked with over the years didn't seem to grasp the concept of driving within oneself and only driving at 80%. For these people who struggle with this concept, I will have them write a memo, mimicking life a little bit and giving them a taste of what would happen on the road if they so happened to misjudge a space and take a mirror off while passing a stopped vehicle. Just like them not making it to the call, I will have them write a memo for hitting a cone. In other words, there are consequences for one's actions.

Good and Bad of Creating Competition

It's my experience that competition is something that the majority of people, who are attracted to the emergency responder's field, have grown up with. They have either been in high-level team sports or high-level academics. Either way, they know what competition is, or in fact, some people thrive on it.

Competition is something that can be a dual-edged weapon; it can either be used for good or used for evil, depending on which instructor is working today...

When I first began driving on performance tracks and was in a race car, I was actually pretty good, but truth be told, I was pretty good only until I was trying to shave off those final few tenths of a second, which ultimately separates the men from the boys. Unfortunately, I would often crumble like an oatmeal cookie as my car was careening off the track, having been unable to handle the pressure.

The same thing happens when we are training at the track. A great deal of my experience has been training anywhere from two to four students at a time on a cone course. I always begin the training without mentioning the stopwatch or even letting the students see me with the watch. I simply teach them the course, provide feedback so that they are performing better, and then I let them practice—in the same way, day in and day out. How the day progresses is dictated by how the instructor sets the stage. If the demonstration by the instructor is at a controlled pace, and the instructor provides appropriate and timely tips highlighting the specific techniques throughout the demonstration, the students most likely will perform well and progress relatively smoothly.

The first step, the student will learn the course; then they will improve their technique and ultimately gain a little bit of confidence. Then I will introduce the stopwatch to them and ask them to give me the quickest but cleanest time. Without a doubt, most times, they will fail and strike a few cones. Okay, good—now they found the limit. The next run, I will ask them to give me a quick run but ensure that they are clean and do not strike a cone. It's amazing how successful they become. If by chance, one or two of the students has a significantly better skillset; this will often be a detriment to the others. Why? Because they will be trying to drive at a level for which they are not ready. Once they start hitting cone after cone, it is very difficult to regain their confidence. Remember that the ego is a very fragile thing, especially the male ego. If this begins to happen, it's always the fault of the instructor—and yes, that means me!

Some days, if these students appear to be a little cocky, my demonstration will be very (purposely) quick and efficient, and therefore challenging the student to push a little bit more. To be totally honest, and to let you see behind the curtain, I am setting them up for failure. In most cases, they are not ready to go at that speed, and definitely not without efficiency. Once they start hitting cones, they will then start to pay attention to the instructors. If I go very slowly on my demonstration, and talk them through each and every point, there's a good possibility these drivers will be able to accomplish the task with very little effort. However, they most likely will never reach their potential; reason being that they didn't even have to try, and yet they performed a clean run.

Competence vs Confidence

When I was working at the police college, I remember my boss saying to me one day: "I don't get many phone calls from chiefs of police who have an officer who has difficulty backing into parking spots, but I do get the calls when an officer is driving continually at 120km/h in 60 km/h zones.

Now, to put this into context, what he was referring to was that not many officers are going to be injured or found liable if they aren't very proficient with driving a car. However, if someone feels that they are invincible and can drive at whatever speeds because they're the greatest gift to driving, then these people pose a risk to themselves, their colleagues, and their organization.

That just goes to reinforce the study from the early 70s, which stated that advanced driver training just leads to more crashes. Personally, I don't agree with this study, nor do I disagree with this study. There is a line between confidence and competence, and this comes into play in a couple of different areas.

Most notably, during track training, drivers can often develop a certain level of overconfidence while being on a track; and therefore, that may bleed into their on-road driving skillset as well.

Drivers who have a high level of skill on the track, must really be taught to incorporate the 80% rule to their driving. We have to spend a great deal of time explaining to them that they are in a controlled environment here, with no opposing traffic, no cross traffic, and therefore we have minimized any potential hazards. Get them to compare that to an on-road environment, where we have very little control over other drivers and/or hazards. With these drivers, it will be very important that we are diligent as instructors, and help them with their decision-making abilities. We will discuss a risk assessment tool later on in the book.

On the other hand, we have the driver who may be very intimidated at higher speeds, or even with a cone layout itself. In these cases, the instructors will need to spend a great deal of time in building confidence as they develop more competence. As an experienced instructor, you have probably already experienced or witnessed a driver who has a decent skill level but who was afraid of making mistakes. For this person, we need to be really encouraging and show them that they do have the ability to push a little harder. As a professional Instructor, you should be asking yourself the question: What comes first, confidence or competence?

I would argue that it is on a situational basis. Based on my experience, I would say that that we need to incrementally improve one piece at a time. In some situations, we have to spend more time increasing our drivers' competence; while in other situations, we need to focus on building our drivers' confidence. Ideally, a driver will improve with their skillset (competence) under your instruction, and will develop some confidence under the tutelage of their field training officer.

False Sense of Safety

I opened this chapter up by saying that track training is my favourite part of driver training, on a track/cone course. That is still true because it is the most fun; but is that where I have the most impact on a new emergency response driver? No, it isn't!

This may be my happy place, with the sun shining and a gentle breeze blowing the trees, with a piece of asphalt splitting the green grass to the horizon. Who am I kidding? If you've ever worked on a skid pad or on a track, you know it's always cold and it's always windy, and it seems like it's always raining... Even with all that said, I still love training on a track.

The problem with track training is that it is unrealistic. Generally, it's because we always conduct training with the vehicles going in the same direction and with little to no cross traffic. There are little to no traffic lights, there are no pedestrians, and there are no blind intersections—in fact, there are often very few intersections to deal with. It has been my experience that being in this environment is very much like operating in a vacuum. Nothing else can get to us!

I find that on many race tracks, there will be a sign on the exit road to the city streets, and it will say something to the effect of: The track is behind you—Please Slow Down and Obey the Traffic Laws on the roadways ahead.

As soon as you read that sign, it automatically separates the track from the road, but as an instructor, it is our job to tie the road driving to the track driving. At least I hope it has been...

I've conducted emergency response training on a track and on a road, and I can tell you that road training is 100% better than track training.

If I want to make a difference and help to reduce the number of officers lost while driving their patrol vehicles, I need to focus more attention to the road. I know that that little voice inside of your head is saying that we don't do that or we can't do that. I want you to start silencing that little voice, and take an objective look at the next chapters. Besides, if you're like me, you're sick and tired of hearing people say, "But that's the way we've always done it; we've never done it that way before." Blah, blah, blah.

Chapter 6

Four Stages of Competence

evoctrainer.com

"You must have confidence in your competence."
– Elijah Cummings

The Psychology of How We Learn

There are many licensed drivers on the road today that are unaware that they are in fact a poor, or shall we say, a substandard driver. This goes the same for recruits that may enter the Police College/Academy who might think they are excellent drivers but in fact are lacking some of the basic skills required.

Sometime in the mid-60s, psychologists created a chart that highlights the "Four Stages of Competence." Sometimes it is referred to as the "Four Stages of Learning a New Skill." I'm okay if you utilize either name.

The Four Stages are:

- Stage One, Unconscious Incompetence: You don't know what you don't know.
- Stage Two, Conscious Incompetence: You now know what you didn't know.

Emergency Vehicle Operation Instruction

- Stage Three, Conscious Competence: You know and you are working toward learning that skill.
- Stage Four, Unconscious Competence: You don't even think about it anymore.

(Please refer to the chart, figure 1 below.)

Four Stages of Competence

Conscious Competence	Unconscious Competence
3rd Stage	4th Stage
Working to improve skill	Habitual skill
Conscious Incompetence	**Unconscious Incompetence**
2nd Stage	1st Stage
Aware of driving errors	Unaware of driving errors

Figure 1

This is where understanding the four stages of competence could be of use to EVO instructors. It has been my experience that two of the most typical driving behaviours that new officer's/cadet's exhibit, are driving too fast and following too closely. Let's start with following too closely, and work that driving behaviour through the four stages of competence.

Unconscious Incompetence

In stage one, the cadet often doesn't recognize that they are too close to the car in front until it is pointed out to them, or worse, they crash into the vehicle in front. It would be nice if you just pointed this out to someone and that was all that they needed to correct a behavior, but that's unrealistic. In this stage, it's a good idea to discuss the problems associated with travelling so close to the vehicle in front. This is the perfect opportunity to start discussing the importance of having a good eye lead for an Emergency Vehicle Operator. Most likely, they are aware, through theory lessons, that the driver should be looking somewhere in the area of 10 to 20 seconds ahead of them, but in reality, what does that look like? This is a great opportunity for you to tie the follow distance and eye-lead pieces together so that they can recognize that these two concepts are interrelated.

Your student will often become defensive when you are discussing the driving behaviours that you have noted in stage 1. This will be normal; just think about when you're discussing something with your children, and how they automatically get defensive and try their best to defend their actions–it's no different in this situation.

Before you are ready to move them into stage number two, so that they are consciously trying the new skill, you must first find a way to get the student to buy into what you are trying to teach them. If they are a willing participant in this process, it will be a much smoother journey for those involved.

Conscious Incompetence

In the second stage of competence, they are now aware of their driving deficiency. Once they have been instructed on how to go about calculating the proper minimum following distance of 2 seconds, they should be able to correct the situation with concentrated effort. Earlier, in stage 1, you identified the problems with following too closely. Now, in this stage, it is important to show them the benefits of having a good following distance. Once again, beginning with an increased eye lead allows them to scan further ahead; and therefore, they should be able to get information in a timelier manner. Take it from me; this won't help in getting the student to buy into your suggestions. In situations like this, I like to incorporate something that is very job-specific. Keeping a minimum 2-second following distance will allow the Emergency Vehicle Operator the opportunity to deal with other tasks (e.g., look for an address, listen to the radio, key a license plate into the computer, or scan the environment for suspects), all while not having to give too much attention to the vehicle in front. An increased following distance will allow the officer to give time to the policing task (more about multi-tasking in just a moment).

I find that most often my students will know that they should be trying for a minimum 2 seconds for a following distance; however, when it comes time to apply this to their own road behaviour, they really have no clue what two seconds actually looks like. It normally comes down to one of two problems: They are using an object off to the side of the road, and it is skewing their perception, or they are just counting too fast.

My preference is that the reference point is always on the road. And it could either be a line crosswalk or a crack, or sometimes even a dip in the road. When the vehicle in front passes set object, I begin to count out loud—one thousand and one, one thousand and two—and once I finish saying two, my car should be crossing the same mark. It may seem strange that I am mentioning how to calculate following distance, in a book for advanced instructors, but I can say that when I first became an instructor, I spent a great deal of time counting to 2 while the supervisor instructor was working the stopwatch. I admit that I have also done the same when I am training new instructors as well.

Stage two is where the instructor works the most. This stage will require a theory lesson, instruction, demonstration, and coaching—lots and lots of coaching. A student will often get frustrated in stage 2, much like my cousin did when learning to drive a standard transmission, as I discussed in Chapter one. Be sure to let the student know that they must be patient with themselves, and that with some dedicated (conscious) practice, they will be certain to improve. With the student understanding that this will take some time and that it is "normal" for new officers to have to adopt new habits for the policing world, they will become a willing participant.

Conscious Competence

In stage number 3, the onus is now on the student to start to develop this new skill, or in other words, modify their behaviour. They already know that they are prone to making this driving error, and they know what is required to fix it. If they're honest with themselves, they will be able to develop this skill without a great deal of instructor intervention.

When I was training new instructors at the police college, we would often conduct on-road training with each other prior to the recruits attending the college. During one of these orientation drives, I had three police officers on board with me as I facilitated from the right front seat. One of the three officers was having difficulty in coming to a complete stop at stop signs. In fact, I don't believe he ever fully stopped for a stop sign, except if another vehicle was coming across our path. When I pointed this out to my driver, he simply laughed it off and said, "I am stopping." The next couple of stop signs, he tried to stop but continued to roll them. I asked him to pull over to the side of the road, and then turned to the two in the back seat and asked for their observations. Both of them confirmed my point that he was not stopping at the stop signs. This particular officer thought that we three were all in on this and were simply pranking him. I didn't realize that this was what he thought until the following week when he came into the office and announced to everyone, "Holy crap, I don't stop at stop signs!" It was like this great epiphany had hit him over the weekend. At least now, he recognized it; and it was now up to him to fix the problem. If you talk to him now, he would readily admit that it took a great deal of conscious thought to force himself to come to full stops at stop signs.

Now let's get back to our student with the following-distance issue. As they continue to progress and continue counting off 2 seconds of following distance, their brain will start to notice what that space looks like, without always having to count. As an instructor, this might be the time to start introducing a couple of additional tasks. You might have them talk on the radio, or if the radio isn't available, simply engage them in a conversation. This could be about anything; it could be about sports, school, or family—it doesn't matter. What you are really looking for is to see what happens to their following- distance as they are engaged in a conversation. Are they able to maintain that minimum two seconds, or are they falling back into their old habits of being too close to the vehicle in front? It's most likely that you will note that when they are distracted, they will revert back to being too close; so therefore, it's an opportunity for you to bring their attention, from whatever conversation you're having, back to the driving so that they can recognize that they have not built this new habit of having a minimum two- second following distance.

This might be a good place to discuss multitasking. This is a term that is often used in policing, and it is especially useful when it comes to driving. There is a great debate amongst the educational theorists and the neuroscientists as to whether it should be known as multitasking or attention switching. Although I am not a neuroscientist, I do believe that it is attention switching that is going on very quickly. In the example we are working through with the driver who follows too closely, we can see that as soon as we distracted them with a conversation, they simply reverted back to their old habits, because they were unable to give attention to both the conversation and the driving task. It is clearly obvious that this driver is still in the conscious competence stage, as they have to give targeted focus to the driving task in order to maintain a minimum two-second following distance. Their continued practicing and targeted focus is still required. This simple conversation approach is a great exercise to complete with your driver, and it will give them instant feedback as to where they are in the four stages of competency.

Unconscious Competence

Stage number four is what we should ultimately be striving for with our students and with ourselves. To be totally honest, it's most likely that you will never witness your driver student driving their car in this stage. It may take months of targeted practice as they progress through phase 3—and let's be honest; there's a good possibility that some drivers will never make it to the fourth stage.

If you went online and looked up the four stages of competence, there's a good chance that people will use the example of driving an automobile as being in the 4th stage of competence. In fact, there's a good chance that you've been thinking the same thing throughout this chapter. As a professional instructor, you should be breaking the driving task down into smaller modules, and not make it one big task as the average person might do. Another example of being in stage 4 is when someone is driving a standard automobile. Usually, someone doesn't have to think about when it's time to change the next gear; they seem to just do it automatically. Hopefully, you now understand that it took targeted and continued practice to get to that level. What would happen if we had a new recruit, driving standard, and tasked them to try to talk on the radio? There's a good possibility that the message would be missed, or that they would fail to engage the clutch as they were coming to a stop sign because they were being overwhelmed by the policing task. Many years ago, I actually did an experiment, and we did the opposite; we had a driver who was unable to attention switch between driving and policing. They were unable to attention switch between accelerating smoothly while encountering a vehicle merging into their lane—often, they would simply put the brakes on rather than move to a new lane to facilitate a merging vehicle. So we introduced a standard-shift vehicle into our training. This was for some private training that we conducted for an officer who was in jeopardy of being terminated because they were unable to drive. We felt that introducing this officer to a standard-shift automobile might force him to read traffic sooner, as well as to develop a better feel for the automobile. Fast forward a few weeks, and this student was able to drive a standard-shift car, albeit not very proficiently given all of the nuances involved; however, he was able to start off on a hill without stalling, and was able to go from point A to point B. Once he attained this level of proficiency, we put him into an automatic transmission vehicle and started to improve his attention switching between driving and the policing task. At the end of the seven or eight weeks of training that we spent with him, he was proficient enough to meet the college and police vehicle operations standards, and to the best of my knowledge, he has had a successful career as an officer; however, I don't think I would ever ask him to be a part of my training cadre of instructors.

Stage 4 is where you ultimately want all your students to get to, at whatever skill you have introduced them to. You should also be striving to be performing in stage four of competency as well. During some Follow Me exercises that we do in live traffic on city streets, I will drive the suspect vehicle as well as be the dispatch while students try to catch up with me and provide a marker, as well as speeds, direction of travel, road conditions, etc. The communication aspect of this exercise takes a great deal of my attention away, as I have to give them the appropriate responses to their questions, and ensure that they are performing at an appropriate level. What do you think this does to my driving? Sometimes I am so consumed with what the students are doing that I'm not even aware (conscious) of my driving, but once I put my conscious attention back to it, I am pleased to report that I have a good following distance and have not allowed anyone to linger beside my vehicle. In other words, even though I was distracted with the policing tasks, I was still able to drive appropriately and leave the appropriate escape spaces around my vehicle—unconscious competence!

Applying This to Your Training

I have used following distance as an example throughout this chapter on the four stages of competency. I hope that as you have been reading this, you have been thinking about other skills for which you could use the four stages of competency to your benefit. This could be used both on the city streets and on a driver training track. How about proper lines of travel and cornering, trying to get your student to only place one demand on the contact patch (tire) at any one time?

Benefits for the student are that they know exactly where they are in the learning cycle, and where to put their attention in order to develop their skills. As an instructor, it allows you to have a dialogue with your student, and together, the two of you can develop a plan of how to go about transitioning from stage 1, all the way to stage 4. As explained earlier in the book, a plan is very important, and sharing that plan with the student will help to ensure success.

If I think back to when I was teaching novice drivers, it never ceased to amaze me that parents would often struggle with trying to teach their children to drive. If we applied this to the context of the four stages, you will recognize that the parent is in stage 4, and doesn't know how to break the driving task down into bite-size modules, like a driving instructor or a professional EVO instructor. Think about where your driver is in the four stages, and plan your training accordingly in order to help them move toward stage number 4.

Hopefully, you've been thinking how you can apply this in your own EVO training with your students. I hope that you can recognize the importance of ensuring that when officers are driving quickly, the basics of space and visibility must be thoroughly applied. More specifically, their basic driving habits must be at a very high level, and ultimately should be in stage 4 of competency prior to responding to emergency calls.

If that indeed is the case, then you can apply multitasking—or as I like to say, attention switching demand (cognitive)—on your officers, because that's exactly what will happen once they get out onto the road. It is your hope as an EVO instructor that your students will be able to drive flawlessly even though they are listening to the radio, trying to plan a route, and figuring out what they're going to do once they arrive upon a scene.

Chapter 7

Foundation of Expert Driving - Eye Placement

"The only source of knowledge is experience."
– Albert Einstein

Do We Really See With Our Eyes?

Can you remember back to when we were children, and we would say to each other ,see with your eyes, not with your hands? Well, these days, I use a slightly different term: We see with our minds, not with our eyes! For many of you, this isn't a completely foreign thought, because you already know this to be true; but let's delve just a little deeper into this concept.

I am not going to begin telling you how the eye works by breaking it down into the different parts, like the iris, cornea, pupil, etc. I am merely going to explain the importance of proper vision skills when it comes to the art of driving.

I'm going to let you in on a little secret right now before we get to the end of the book. A great deal of conversation and training surrounds the concept of experience. Yes, the concept of gaining experience will undoubtedly help someone learn a new skill, such as manoeuvering the steering wheel, or applying the appropriate pressure to the brake pedal to ensure that we don't end up with our seat belt locking, and developing the skill to accelerate smoothly so as to avoid giving our passengers whiplash. Yes, I agree that experience helps all of said skills become more habitual, but what about their minds, and creating experiences through which your students can draw upon?

When I speak about experience, it isn't necessarily about what the hands and feet are doing, but more about what the mind is doing. Is it starting to develop file folders within our brains, storing tens of thousands, if not millions, of pieces of data? I will often send some of my more problematic students on a homework quest. Their quest will often involve driving in a different environment, and perhaps even in a city where they have never been before. What I am trying to do is get them to log many more miles of experience, which will help them develop the mental processing to driving an automobile at a much higher level of proficiency.

The human eye itself is attracted to movement and light, or more specifically, contrast. Fact: The average driver will proceed down the road and not move their eyes until something attracts their attention; then and only then, the driver will make a decision and react to the stimuli.

As professional instructors, we all know that a driver must move their eyes every two or three seconds in order to continually process the driving scene. As we approach a controlled intersection, we know that a driver should look at the traffic lights to see which colour it is, and the colour of the light will dictate what decision we make. If it's green, we are proceeding through; if it's amber, we're going to stop, etc. If we go one step further and look at that exact same intersection, if the light is green, where should we look? I would hope that we would be looking to see if there are any vehicles about to make a left hand turn across our path—that particular vehicle is one that we have nicknamed *"a sniper."* In other words, a vehicle that is hiding or is perhaps camouflaged behind other vehicles, waiting to make a left turn in our direction of travel, and we do not see them until they make a move to turn either in front of us or into us. They were waiting to pick us off, just like a sniper would wait to take the shot.

A skilled driver will have trained themselves to habitually inspect the intersection on a green light, for potential threats—most notably, the *sniper,* who's about to turn left across our path. That is our job as an instructor; to help our students develop a habitual scanning pattern, which will help them to be a proactive driver as opposed to a reactive driver.

Importance of Peripheral Vision

If we could all agree that a person has approximately 180 degrees of forward visibility—some would have a little bit more, some perhaps little bit less—for our purposes, we will use the number 180 degrees. This is sometimes termed *field of view*. Of the 180 degrees of forward visibility, 5 to 6 degrees is what is known as central vision; in other words, that's what we are focussed on, such as a sign or a car, etc. That leaves approximately 175 degrees of vision, which is more commonly known as peripheral vision. Yes, I'm aware that you have near, mid, and fringe vision, but for our purposes, we will simply call all of it peripheral vision. Our peripheral vision is where we notice contrast (colour) and movement. In fact, if we were looking for something in low level light or at night, it would be best to avoid using our central vision, and allow the peripheral to seek out movement.

Why is peripheral vision so important to driving, you might ask? First of all, that is the vision that allows us to stay centered within our lane. We don't want our drivers looking down at the dotted line with their central vision. We want them to get their eyes up off the road, looking toward the horizon, and allowing the peripheral to guide them. When I'm teaching in a classroom and trying to get my students to understand the importance of peripheral vision, I will often use the analogy of when they're walking from their living room into their kitchen. They don't have to stop and suddenly inspect the door frame to ensure that they can safely traverse from one room to the next; they simply know that they will fit between that door frame, and their peripheral vision will guide them through. Driving down the road, we don't have to inspect the surface or look at the car to our left or right; our peripheral will guide us between the dotted lines. The same can be said for parking spots; we simply aim our central vision through the centre of the spot, and our peripheral will guide us between the vehicles.

One phenomenon of the human eyes and brain is that we will often move in the direction in which we are looking, which on one hand is a good strategy for driving, but on the other can be quite dangerous. Have you ever noticed that a vehicle that has lost control and gone off the road into a field, manages to find the only tree around for miles? That's probably because when the driver left the road, their eyes automatically started searching for what they were going to hit; or in other words, what was going to hurt the most. It is the same with a city collision; quite often, the vehicle has left the road and crashed into the only structure available—the bus shelter. Why? Because that was where the driver was looking; therefore, they steered the vehicle right into it. More often than not, you'll find that the point of impact is directly in the centre of the front bumper.

Tunnel Vision

Tunnel vision is a term we often use in Emergency Vehicle Operation training, but do we truly understand what this phenomenon is and how it is created? Tunnel vision is where our peripheral vision tightens closer to the proximity of our central vision; in other words, our vision and overall awareness is lessened. How does this occur? If we keep it clearly in the confines of driving, it can happen because you do not move your eyes either left or right; it happens as our speed increases, and it also happens if we are processing difficult cognitive information. Oh yes, then there is this other phenomenon known as stress. All of these different factors can lead to a driver developing tunnel vision.

In other words, tunnel vision only occurs if certain conditions are present, and they include a plethora of information overloading our senses, either visual or auditory. It could also occur as their speed is increasing, and will occur when their physiological state is being heightened by stress. Now do you see the problem here? These are all factors that can be acting upon Emergency Vehicle Operators at any given point in time.

Now the question is: What do we do about tunnel vision, and how do we manage it?

Correlation Between Speed and Vision

Okay, so we just discussed what tunnel vision is, and we talked about some of the cognitive factors that influence tunnel vision. I'd like to focus on speed, and more importantly, the correlation between speed and vision. I hear instructors talk about tunnel vision—as you go faster, it starts to tighten—but I sometimes wonder if they really understand just how significant a reduction of vision is present as speeds go up. In the accompanying chart (Figure 2), you can see that just by increasing the speed from 0 to 65kph (41mph), we have already lost 80 degrees of our *useful field of view*. This chart only goes to 100kph (62mph), but you can appreciate that the UFOV would be considerably smaller as the speeds get over 130kph (80mph).

Refer to the chart below, Figure 2

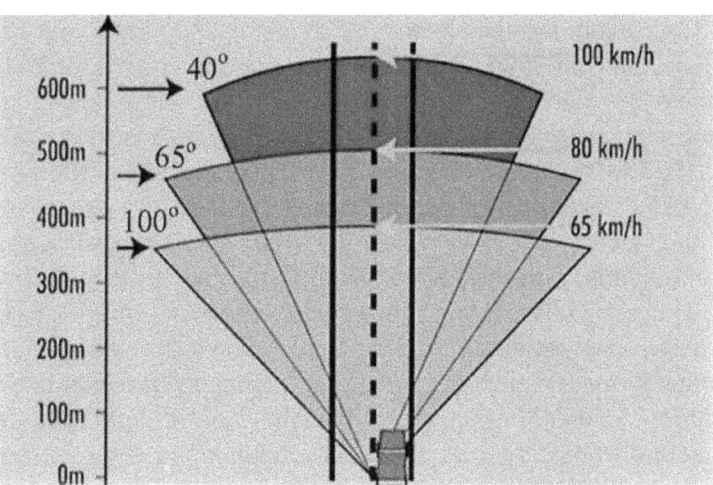

Figure 2

Looking Through the Corner

If you take the heading of this section literally, you might think that I'm speaking of crystal balls and sorcery but I will leave that to Harry Potter. That's not what this book is about.

I'm talking about trying to get a driver's eye-lead as far up the road as they can see; in fact, some may even say to the vanishing point, but in reality, that is probably a little too far in some situations.

When approaching a corner, there are three main components to each corner: braking, turn in, and acceleration out. As EVO instructors, we spend a great deal of time on this, and we must ensure that we help our students develop good seeing habits in all three of these components.

Projecting your eyes well ahead will help to recognize the shape of the corner, and should dictate the speed at which you want to enter the corner. Additionally, you will need to know how much you can see beyond the apex. If not far, the speeds will be kept low, but if you have good sight lines, you could go faster through the corner. A tight on-ramp is a good example where you might not see the apex or know what's behind it; however, an on-ramp is also a great place to practice projecting your eye lead further up the road, and having your hands follow your eyes. If you do this through a corner, the platform of the vehicle will generally be very balanced and will enable earlier, smoother acceleration.

If a driver is to continually be looking over the nose of the vehicle, or looking down at the ground, they will usually instill a sawing effect on the steering wheel. I am sure that most of you can relate to this phenomenon, especially when it comes to track driving. When you are discussing this or riding with a student during normal driving such as being on city streets or in a parking lot, do you remind your driver to look farther through the corner? You probably have mentioned it when it's raining, or if you have had the experience of riding with someone while it's snowing, but do you work on their visual habits during normal, low-risk driving tasks?

It's my observation that most drivers do not look in the proper spot when they make a normal turn, left or right. More often than not, when making a left-hand turn, they will look back to the right shoulder to see what is coming toward them; in other words, what did they just turn in front of? This is a bad habit to be in, because there's no more risk coming up; it's too late. The risk that is approaching is to the front of the intended path of your vehicle, which is why we spend so much time talking about looking through the corner where you want to get to.

The same thing happens when people make right-hand turns onto a roadway; they will glance back over the left shoulder to see what's coming—once again, too late! The vision needs to be out in front of the vehicle, especially in poor weather conditions where the driver needs to be looking to the horizon should there be a requirement to fix a skid. I can tell you for a fact that many collisions involving a police vehicle rear-ending a civilian driver, on right turns, is happening because the officer isn't looking forward where they want to go; they're looking the wrong way because that is their general habit when making turns.

If we spend so much time working on proper cornering technique and eye lead through corners when we are working on a track or cone course, then wouldn't it make sense that we spend just as much time working on visual skills during the basics of driving? This is the foundation or cornerstone of good defense driving. If your driver is looking in the right spot during normal basic driving tasks, you have a far better chance of getting them to look to the right place when driving in a more assertive manner.

Proper Scanning Techniques

If we want our drivers to avoid tunnel vision, then we must give them a strategy that will help them overcome and/or limit the detrimental effects that may occur.

Based on the previous sections, we now understand that the entire field of view starts to restrict itself, and instead of the vision field operating at a hundred and eighty degrees, it now may only be working at 100°. We also agree that peripheral vision is the critical field of view; therefore, we must find ways to increase its range.

How do we do that? Simple: We teach our drivers to scan. Scanning means looking to the extreme left and extreme right of our field of view, as well as taking in part of the rear view as well.

How far to the left and right do we actually look? My students often tell me I am scanning, as I watch them they are moving their eyes to the left and they're moving their eyes to the right and this may work well as we are travelling down the road at 50kph (25 mph) but what is going to happen as the speed increases? Will my driver understand the effect that speed is having on their vision? I doubt it, so this time it's imperative to get drivers to move their heads and scan to the left all the way to a physical barrier, whether its buildings, guard rails, or a tree line. We need to expand their vision, and the same goes when scanning to the right all the way out to a physical barrier—buildings, guard rails, or tree lines.

There's an exercise that I have my student complete, where they drive down a slow-speed, four-lane roadway, with two lanes travelling in each direction. I ask them to point out any child under the age of 10 who is in the environment but not inside a vehicle. I know that within the first few minutes of their drive, there is a nursery school on the right-hand side of the road, and 7 out of 10 drivers will not notice the children playing behind the fence—the children are no more than 40 feet from the roadway, but for some reason, the drivers do not scan or look deep enough to find the threats. Okay, these 4 and 5-year- olds aren't really threats, but you get the point. The drivers are not in the habit of scanning that far off the roadway, and they are not turning their head enough when they scan. If you think back to the chart that highlights the correlation of speed and visibility, what happens to our "useful field of visibility?" It gets narrower as we increase speed; therefore, we need to move our heads as we scan, and it will move our UFOV. If done correctly, our UFOV could be at 130 degrees, even at 80kph, if we move our head and in turn expand our UFOV.

We spend a great deal of time getting our drivers to actively scan, or in other words, move the head from left to right, and visually inspect physical barrier to physical barrier while travelling relatively slow speeds. The intention is to keep pushing that skill onto them, and asking them to practice scanning in their own vehicle. Ultimately, we want them to turn this into a habit; or more importantly, we want scanning to be at a level at which we now know to be unconsciously competent, even as speeds increase.

Chapter 8

Commentary Driving

evoctrainer.com

"Change is the law of life. And those who look only to the past or present are certain to miss the future."
– John F. Kennedy

What Is it?

Have you ever ridden in the backseat of a cab or an Uber, and the driver just wouldn't stop talking? Well, commentary is nothing like that... Okay, maybe it is, because it can be extremely annoying to the uninitiated.

A *commentary drive*, sometimes known as a *narrative drive*, is nothing brand new and has been around for decades. There are some old videos of Harold Smith conducting commentary in the 50s and 60s. The London Metropolitan Police have been using commentary driving for years as well. It has been around for a great deal of time, and I by no means am the inventor; however, I am a huge proponent of the value of incorporating commentary driving into someone's training.

It is simply a process where the driver describes what they are seeing as they proceed down the road. Basic Drivers Education teaches drivers to continually scan sidewalk to sidewalk, and to not forget to check the mirrors. These drivers may be scanning, but they have no idea what they should be looking for or where they should be looking, or for that matter, when to look there.

The commentary drive will help someone, with proper coaching, develop an extraordinary scanning process, which ultimately needs to become habitual for them.

When I first began my advanced instruction career at the Skid Control School, I had an opportunity to take my mother out for some training on the skid pad. It is a great memory for me, even though I don't think that she learned anything from being on the skid pad that day, but she sure had a lot of fun! Considering that the skid pad was located about a 30-minute drive from where she lived, I did take the opportunity to conduct a commentary drive as I drove her home. She was so enthralled with the information that I was providing, that she actually was driven to tears. Keep in mind that this was my mother, and of course she had to be pleased, but it may actually have come down to her being thankful that I actually had a real job and was no longer strapping myself into race cars. Having said that, she wasn't the first person to tell me that they received more relevant and useful information during a commentary driving session than during a skid pad session.

As instructors, our ultimate goal is to help our students become the best drivers that they can be. If you can get your student to develop an excellent scanning pattern by incorporating commentary into your lessons, the student is much better positioned to move their scanning process into stage four. In other words, to become unconsciously competent.

How Does It Work?

On the face of it, commentary driving is a very simple exercise to help build a proper scanning pattern. The reality is, doing it at a high level with appropriate and timely scanning takes a great deal of practice. A good starting point for commentary driving is the understanding that there are three looks to the front of the vehicle, plus one look to the rear, and to simply keep repeating the process.

I am open to two scanning patterns: left, center, and right, plus to the rear; or my preferred pattern of left, right, straight, and then to the rear. As the old saying goes, six of one or a half dozen of the other— it's all the same thing. Please use whichever one you see as being more appropriate.

One of the most common mistakes when incorporating commentary driving into your training is allowing the student to talk about things that are historical in nature, or more specifically, when the driver talks about things that have just occurred instead of talking about things in the future. The goal of commentary driving is to support an eye-lead of 15–20 seconds away, and to develop a scanning pattern of a physical barrier to the left and a physical barrier to the right, and then what is happening behind the vehicle.

Commentary can be used on a closed course as well. This would help train your drivers to be proactive with their eyes, and will also slow them down just a little bit. Here's another secret for you: Often, drivers will find that conducting a commentary drive gets confusing, and they most likely will be talking historically. In other words, they most likely can't keep up. That's a good thing, because now you can have them slow down, and help them to develop the commentary.

If a driver is being overwhelmed while conducting a commentary drive, it probably means that they are driving faster than what their brain can process. I challenge you to play with this process a little bit, but I think you will quickly see the benefits of slowing a driver down when you are training them.

Bottom-Up vs Top-Down Processing

If you happen to be a psychology major or a neuroscientist, you are about to become very disappointed, because I am going to take a little creative license here and dumb things down a bit. According to neuroscientists, bottom-up processing is having an external stimulus— what your eye sees to begin the process. Whereas bottom-down processing is where your perception, also known as experience, helps to fill in the gaps and make a decision. Top-down processing is based on your experience and perceptions, telling your eyes to inspect the left turn lane because of the probability that most risk at this intersection will be coming from there. If that is already in your mind, you know that you have two avenues of escape: move to the right to be better seen, or brake. Okay, okay, there is a third; if the person is truly committed to making their turn, then yes, you should be ready to steer to the rear.

Earlier in the book, we discussed how the eye works, and we also made mention that the majority of drivers will not move their eyes in search of hazards but will simply wait until the eye catches movement or contrast. Then they will put their attention to whatever just caught their eye, and then decide if it is a hazard; and if so, what steps can the driver do to mitigate any risk from that hazard? Will they need to slow down, change lanes, or even accelerate? This phenomenon could be known as bottom-up processing. We allowed the information to grab our eyes' attention, and then we ran it through the filter up to the brain, and await its decision on what action we should take. This is a very rudimentary, or as I like to say, novice approach, to the driving task. The driver needs to be proactive in order to traverse the modern day traffic, especially an Emergency Vehicle Operator.

What does an advanced driver look like on the road? Some definitions would undoubtedly include aware, smooth, proactive, etc. The only way for a driver to be aware, proactive, and smooth is for them to be looking well ahead into their future, in predicting what may or may not be happening ahead of them. An experienced driver will have to develop a proper scanning pattern, which starts at the top and works its way down. When approaching a green traffic light that has been green for a little bit, an experienced driver's brain will tell them to inspect for a vehicle looking to turn left across their path. If one presents itself, and the driver has already anticipated that the left turner may be coming out toward them, part of the decision process has already been made, and the driver is able to either position the vehicle to the right or is applying the brakes and reducing speed. Then the brain will tell the eyes to look to the cross street or driveways on the right, in search of potential hazards.

Benefits of Commentary for the Driver

There are a few different ways in which commentary driving benefits the driver:

It allows them to process information on a deeper level, with the intention that they will have a better memory of said info for later.

It provides them with an actual plan as to how scanning should be conducted.

In most cases, it will cause the driver to actually reduce their speed in order to keep up with the commentary. From my perspective, and based on the thousands of students I've ridden with, this is not a bad thing.

During my time as a volunteer working with adults learning to read, I was able to develop my knowledge base in regard to how we learn, and more specifically, how we process information. Do you remember when you were learning to read, or perhaps when you were helping your child learn to read? It was always best if they read out loud, and that way you could help them with proper pronunciation. A recent study showed that reading out loud can have significant benefit for us retaining the information. I know what you are thinking—we should have more audiobooks—but actually, more recent studies have indicated that it's better to hear the information in your own voice. So reading it out loud is still superior to an audiobook. So how does this come into play for EVO instructors? This is an opportunity to explore the benefits of commentary for the driver: Helping the driver develop a habitual scanning pattern will serve them for the rest of their driving careers. Teaching someone to look at the right spot at the right time will undoubtedly save lives.

Benefits for the Instructor

Whenever I introduce commentary driving to the field training officers, they always give a loud sigh of relief. They believe that commentary driving benefits them the most by letting them know what the driver is seeing; therefore, it will allow them to be a little less on edge. I have to admit that this is in fact one of the key benefits to the person sitting in the right front seat. As an instructor or FTO, you should continually be aware of what the driver is seeing, and therefore what they are doing to mitigate the risk.

Please keep in mind that commentary driving should be incorporated in all aspects of a student driver's training sessions. It should begin on a cone course or even on a track, at slower speeds. As a student gains proficiency with the exercise, as well as commentary, they will be able to proceed to more challenging or advanced training exercises. A slow speed commentary walkthrough of a cone course can quickly evolve into a quick but proficient commentary around the track.

Commentary is probably most useful out on the city streets and in live traffic. As always, the KISS (Keep It Simple Silly) principle should be followed. If your driver has difficulties conducting a commentary while driving down the travelled roadway, they are by no means ready to be conducting emergency response driving exercises, either on track or on the road. This again is something that is often targeted toward the field training officers; if your student can't crawl, let alone walk, then why are you trying to get them to run?

From an EVO instructor perspective, a commentary drive allows you, as an instructor, to model the behaviour by conducting a "model" demonstration drive. I use the term "model" as opposed to "perfect," because I have been unable to conduct a perfect drive, even after more than 25 years. However, it is something that I still strive for every time I conduct a demo drive.

With you modelling the drive to your student, you are showing them the path to be a proficient Emergency Vehicle Operator. They will have been given an insight as to where and when a driver should be looking, at any particular place. You have now set the standard.

Once your driver begins applying the commentary drive, you will be able to very easily distinguish just how far ahead they are looking. Depending on the environment with which you are working, you will want them to be looking anywhere from 8 to 12 to 20 seconds ahead.

A student conducting a commentary drive may gloss right over something that you perceive as being a threat and/or a critical component of the driving task. Right away, you can have them pull the car over safely and have a discussion on that particular component. Having a student conduct a commentary drive may also lead you into recognizing that there are issues that go beyond driving. Case in point: I had a problem driver who I thought was very late in all of their braking when slowing to make changes of direction. In listening to the commentary, I was able to ascertain that the issue was that they were unable to read the street signs in a timely manner. This had nothing to do with driving but simply that they couldn't see because they needed glasses, despite them having 20/20 vision—or so they said. The next day I rode with them, they had glasses, and their braking application was both timely and smooth.

Who knows; listening to someone conduct a commentary drive may actually lead you to learn a new language. I have facilitated the commentary exercise in many different languages, including but not limited to French, Spanish, Punjabi, and Cantonese. Just because your driver struggles to conduct a commentary drive, doesn't necessarily mean that they are unable to drive in a proficient manner. Remember, with all training exercises, there are some students that will be unable to excel at the level you wish, but perhaps you can encourage them to practice commentary driving on their own.

Language Matters

One thing that I have learned in my years of training with people who arrive with various backgrounds and languages, is that sometimes it is not driving skill, or even their decision abilities behind the wheel, that is in question. The truth of the matter is that it is often the nuances of the English language, or worse yet, the nomenclature of policing/EMS, etc.

If someone is preoccupied with trying to figure out what you were saying or asking of them, they will often be a few seconds behind in their information processing and, ultimately, decisions. I have had many students be sent to me, whom others have labelled as being unable to drive, only to realize that the issue isn't driving—it is a language situation, or perhaps the instructor or FTO.

Truth be known, when I first laid out the headings for each chapter, before I began writing the book, I intended to discuss language matters from the instructor's perspective. Perhaps the better topic would have been "words matter." In my early years, I may have asked a student to "go ahead and take that light," meaning that I would like them to come to a stop for the red, and when it is safe to do so, activate the emergency equipment and proceed against the red. My students, however, thought that "take the light" meant to just drive through it without stopping. Yikes! There was a big difference between what the two of us were talking about.

Words we use, whether we are giving instruction or demonstration, must be universally accepted, at least to your organization, and this is when it's imperative that the instructor bridge the gap between the organizational knowledge, and perhaps even the nomenclature to what your student will be bringing in with them.

You must be sure that you are not using colloquialism, unless they have a clear understanding of what you're speaking about. Your instructions also must be timely and consistent, and as an instructor, you need to develop that pattern. Simple instructions, such as having someone take the next left, can be quite different than having your student turn at the next traffic light. You want your driver to develop appropriate decision making when it comes to the driving task. Don't just tell them what to do; you want them to be able to do it for themselves.

Here is an example, which isn't exactly about language, but it's more a tip about instruction and decision-making. I had an opportunity to drive on a track in Ohio, on which I had never really driven before. The instructor, who was buckled in beside me, said, "Okay, Canada, you just do what I tell you, and you're going to look like a star!" All right, perfect, sounds good to me, and off we go. I will admit that I did look pretty good, and I got a lot of great feedback from all the other students and instructors alike at lunch time. After lunch, however, I hopped in with a different instructor, and he said to me,

"Okay, you know what you're doing, so go ahead. I'll just sit here and say something if need be." What a difference. I was too early on the brakes, waiting on the turn in, and ultimately downright slow. Why? Because my first instructor wasn't teaching me; he was merely telling me what to do, and if I was a good student and followed his instructions perfectly, it was therefore really him making all the driving decisions, not me. When it came time for me to make the decisions, I lacked his knowledge and expertise, and was unable to perform at a high level. Now I'm happy to admit that I was able to work myself back up to the high level, but it took some time as I needed to create my own experience and decisions from which I could draw upon later. So I want you to ask yourself: Is it important for your student to do well with you in the car, or do you want your student to do well for the next 30 years?

Chapter 9

Decision Making

evoctrainer.com

"Where there is great power, there is great responsibility."
– Winston Churchill

Mitigating Driving Risk

As mentioned earlier in the book, as an EVO instructor, we know that too many law enforcement personnel are being killed while operating the motor vehicle. What are we doing to change this?

The art of driving an automobile hasn't changed all that much in the past 40 years or so. Yes, vehicle manufacturers have added safety equipment to the vehicles, such as seat belts, anti-lock brakes, electronic stability control, along with airbags. That's what the manufacturers have done, but what about us as EVO instructors? What have we done to improve?

This is a question that has been circulating among professional instructors for many years, probably around a decade. We recognize that the issue lies not so much with driver skill but with the decision making of the driver or operator. What are we doing to help improve their decision making skills?

The term "risk mitigation" is often used with insurance companies, city managers, and chiefs of police, but is it a term that you use during the delivery of your training?

I was listening to Travis Yates, of Tulsa PD, deliver a presentation during a Below-100 class, when he mentioned an email that he had received from a former student. The student wrote to Travis thanking him for teaching him the Shuffle Steer technique, which he claims saved him from a wreck, and he even included the actual dash-cam footage. This video showed the police cruiser running code on a county road that was now entering the city limits. As he entered the city and was approaching a traffic light, there was little to no speed reduction on the part of the officer. The light was green for him, and a vehicle (code name, sniper) was turning left across his path. The officer swerved to the rear and was able to avoid the vehicle with just a couple of fishtails as he regained control. I was dumbfounded; thank goodness Travis spoke about just how shocked he was that the officer hadn't recognised that the environmental factors had drastically changed and demanded a large speed reduction prior to the intersection. Yes, the officer demonstrated good car control; however, his decision making, or failure to recognize the need to reduce speed as he entered the city limits, led to an evasive action that could have been so easily avoided to begin with. It should also be noted that the call he was responding to was already under control by two officers who were on scene.

As professional instructors, we have to do a better job of teaching our students the importance of continually assessing the factors surrounding our call and our associated response to it. Ask yourself: How much time do I spend teaching decision making in my EVO classes? Is it enough? Can I do more?

Decision Making Model N.R.A. (Action Criteria)

As you look at this subtitle, I bet you're wondering what the heck the National Rifle Association has to do with EVO instruction. I am not referring to the National Rifle Association, but I am referring to the *action criteria decision making model*, which asks three questions: Is it **N**ecessary, is it **R**isk effective, and is it **A**cceptable?

In 1989, the FBI academy's Special Operations and Research Unit (S.O.R.U.) looked at three high profile hostage taking incidents that had ended badly. They wanted to see what information was considered, and how it factored into the decision making of the incident commanders and the tactical responders.

Although the three incidents were not identical, there were a number of commonalities, which led the researchers to believe that high risk factors were present in all three of these incidents. At the conclusion of this review, it was their recommendation that whenever high risk factors are present, an action criteria should be considered prior to taking action. In other words, give them a model that will help with their decision making process.

You're probably wondering what a hostage taking incident has to do with Emergency Vehicle Operation instruction. On the other hand, perhaps you were of the mindset that, of course, our drivers are facing high risk factors every time they answer a call for service. This is the exact tool that your students could benefit from. In all honesty, you probably believe that you help your officers develop their decision making by teaching your agency's rules and policy, as well as introducing them to case law and/or supreme court decisions.

Let's look at the different components. First of all, whenever someone is driving a motor vehicle, they must be continually evaluating the visibility, road, weather, and traffic conditions. We should call this the basic principles for driving. What happens once we start layering the demands that are placed upon emergency vehicle operators when they are responding to a call for service?

Some people consider weighing the *perceived risk* versus the *objective risk*. The perceived risk might be something like, "If I don't get to the scene quick enough, my partner/colleague could be injured, if not worse." While the objective risk is, "If I get into a crash, I'm not going to be able to help them at all, and in many cases, I will require assistance myself." Does this sound familiar? Let's give our students a process that they could follow, which will help them in determining which driving action is required of them.

Is It Necessary?

The model begins with the question: Is it necessary? When asking if it is necessary, the first thing we need to be considering is, what exactly is "it?" Is it necessary to speed? Is it necessary to go through that red light? Is it necessary to make that traffic stop, etc.?

Let's run this application of the action criteria through a situation. An officer gets dispatched to a shoplifting call. Is it necessary to go "lights and siren?" What does your policy state regarding this response? The officer actually needs more information than I have provided, so let's add to this. The officer needs to be processing the basic information: Does he/she need to utilize emergency equipment, and will they be required to go through red lights?

"Is it necessary" can mostly be run through your department's policy and/or state regulations on what level of response is required due to the prioritization of the calls. In this particular case, it would depend on whether a shoplifting call is deemed a high priority, and will help decide on whether it is necessary to speed and/or go through a red traffic light. However, we all know that a great deal more goes into the decision on whether this is truly an emergency call.

Additional information might look something like this: A shop owner has detained a shoplifter. The suspect is approximately 11 years old. The call taker can hear yelling and screaming in the background, as well as the girl crying. Is it necessary to speed and exceed the speed limit, and is it necessary to take red lights?

Do we have enough information yet? Let's not forget about the basic driving principles; what is the road weather traffic and visibility conditions like? How about if there is any additional information from the scene; what about weapons, or any other people present?

What is the probable outcome, and what will we be required to do once we arrive? Are there any threats to the safety of any parties involved?

As an EVO instructor, we need to help our students develop their series of questions in order to come to the conclusion that it is necessary to go through red lights and/or speed. The most important piece of the "is it necessary" component, actually comes down to the question: In order to keep people safe and to not put others in harm's way, is it necessary to speed and go through red lights?

At this point in time, you still haven't run it through the full action criteria, because we have two more steps to go.

Is It Risk Effective?

You have all witnessed or have been guilty of taking unnecessary risk while driving to a call or while being involved in a pursuit. Before we continue on with our little case study of the shoplifting call, let's take a moment to discuss the meaning of risk. The Oxford Dictionary defines the term "risk" as a chance or possibility of danger, loss, injury, or other adverse consequences. When we read this, our immediate reaction ascertains that this is a daily occurrence for Emergency Vehicle Operators. That's where our job comes in as an EVO instructor, and we help our officers/students manage that risk effectively. The Oxford Dictionary defines the term "effective" as producing the result that is wanted or intended; the fact of producing a successful result.

In order to proceed to the second stage of the evaluation process, determining if our response is risk effective, we must first agree that we have already deemed this to be a necessary response. For the sake of our discussion here, let's assume that it has passed the necessary phase, and we are now proceeding to: What speed is deemed to be risk effective in your mind? Is it 50% over the speed limit, maybe 100% over the speed limit, or perhaps your policy does not give you an arbitrary number. Does your policy have guidelines for driving left of centre? Does your policy state that you must stop at all red lights prior to proceeding through, or can you reduce speed, and if safe to do so, proceed without stopping? As you were reading these questions, I know that subconsciously you are answering them, but now I would like you to look at all of those questions through the lens of being risk effective.

Your policy may state that officers can drive at whatever speed they wish, provided that their emergency equipment is activated, but is that really an objective way to manage risk? As an EVO instructor, we know the way that drivers see, and we know from experience that not all road users are as aware of their surroundings as we would like them to be; so therefore it may not be managing risk effectively unless we develop additional guidelines for our drivers.

Our students should be considering their perceived risk; in this particular case, the injury to the shop owner versus the objective risk—whom are they placing in harm's way as they go through red lights and drive left of centre?

Now, if we started to factor in the road, weather, visibility, and traffic conditions, perhaps our drivers would come up with a different driving response. On this particular day, we have dry roads with sunny blue skies, and early afternoon, light traffic. The one factor that should be at play is that when it is a bright sunny day, we know it automatically limits the effectiveness of our emergency lights. So, although we may be able to see with clear visibility, we may not be seen as easily as one would expect, due to the bright sunshine. Remember back to the chapter on eyes—we need contrast to grab our attention.

Some of you may be questioning the travelling left of centre tactic. Some may say, as long as you can see if it's clear, then it should be acceptable, while others might say that you should never cross the center line. Personally, I am open to both viewpoints, but they need to be run through the lens of risk effectiveness.

When using the risk effectiveness lens, it may be prudent to pass a slow-moving vehicle (tractor) that is travelling at maybe 10–15 miles per hour. As the pass is being completed, the speed differential between the two vehicles must be very low. Continually assess what the possibility is of the tractor making a turn—are there any laneways, driveways, etc.? What is the shape of the road ahead? Are there any other vehicles present? Once again, we are using risk effectiveness to determine our action criteria in order to complete one manoeuvre—passing a tractor. The accompanying questions to this one are: Is it risk effective to all involved—the public? The police? The subject? Is there a less risky way to do it? This speaks to decision making in regard to pursuits. On an empty rural roadway in good weather, is it risk effective to pursue a 15-year-old who has stolen his parents' car? It is likely risk effective for the public as they are not around. It may be risk effective for the officer, who has a significant amount of driver training and experience, but is it risk effective for the 15-year-old, who is likely new to driving, and whose decision making will be affected by stress. If we apply this to pursuit prevention, PIT, spike belts, etc. What is the least risky way to accomplish our goal (which we have already determined is necessary)?

Is It Acceptable?

We have now made it to the third stage of the action criteria: Is it acceptable?

If something goes wrong and we fail to notice that a cyclist is wearing AirPods and doesn't hear us approaching the red light, and we strike him; or perhaps someone is turning out of their driveway and fails to notice the squad car approaching, having more than doubled the posted speed limit; or perhaps the elderly gentleman who is crossing the street to check his mailbox, failed to notice the speed at which the squad is car approaching—is it acceptable to be travelling at double the speed limit, responding to this shoplifting call? Is it acceptable to go through the red light without stopping? Is it acceptable to be driving left of centre on route to this call? The answer to all of these questions is... It depends! It depends on who we are asking this question of. If we look at the overall driving response to this call, was it acceptable?

When we are talking about your driving response being acceptable, it comes down to three main areas:

Number one: Is it judicially acceptable? Is the officer acting within legal parameters—highway traffic act, criminal code? Is the officer in compliance of the law? It is understood that officers are given exemptions to the law in some circumstances while in the execution of their duties. Speed and red lights are examples, but there are conditions imposed on those exemptions in the name of public safety.

Officers can go through red lights only after coming to a complete stop, ensuring that it is safe, and activating their full emergency equipment. Anything less would be judicially or legally unacceptable.

Number two: Is it civilly acceptable? Specifically, could you be held civilly responsible for the consequences of your driving actions?

Number three: Is it morally acceptable? Perhaps this one is even stronger. Can you go home to your family and tell them at dinner what happened while driving to that shoplifting call? Will that be acceptable to them? Will it be acceptable to you? You will have to live with the consequences of your driving decisions that day.

Although this driving may be acceptable to some on your platoon, it may not be acceptable to your sergeant, your lieutenant, your captain, or your chief. Will this sort of driving response be acceptable to the community?

If we asked the shop owner, who had detained the suspect, he may have said, "Oh yes, that is acceptable. I needed the police to be here quick!" That's only if nothing went wrong. I'm sure the narrative would have looked quite different had someone been killed by a responding police car. Perhaps something like, "It was no big deal; I had everything under control."

Incorporating NRA into Training

It may seem that this little case study that I used for this action criteria example was weak. I chose this example purposely. On the face of it, this may appear to be unrealistic, and you would never need to apply action criteria to a shoplifting call. I can tell you that this happened, and I was a witness to every step of the way that my driver was not applying the NRA action criteria throughout. Let me go back in time, approximately 12–13 years ago.

Part of my role as an EVO instructor is to ride with officers who are relatively new to the road, and then offer tips and suggestions for improvement. These officers would have anywhere between four and twelve months of being solo. I would simply arrive for the morning roll call and spend an entire shift with an officer. On this particular day, we were just clearing the precinct shortly after lunch when the dispatcher requested any available unit to attend a shoplifting call. My officer volunteered to respond to the convenience store. The call was relatively close to us, about 6 or 7 minutes away.

    My driver immediately activated his full emergency equipment as we exited the division, and he accelerated to around 100% over the posted speed limit. In our future was one of the largest intersections in the city. It consisted of three lanes northbound, three lanes southbound, with three lanes of cross traffic in each direction. There were also dual left-turn lanes for all four directions. We were fortunate that traffic was busy enough that it forced him to stop and wait before we could proceed in making a left turn. From then on, the traffic was very minimal. We were getting continual updates through the dispatcher, adding in the information, the screaming, the yelling, and the crying. The screaming and yelling was from the 11-year-old female suspect, who was yelling, "Call my mom." This was all information that I was hearing come across, but I doubted that my driver was taking this in. We turned onto the road with the convenience store on it; it was a residential type road, with a single lane in each direction. We passed two or three vehicles at a speed that necessitated crossing the centerline. The whole time, I'm continually evaluating his driving; I'm looking out for potential threats, and I'm having an internal dialogue with myself—debating on whether I should let him continue, or slow him down and get him to process the information that is coming across the radio.

    We pulled into the lot and stopped directly in front of the doors; we exited the vehicle, and we went into the store. A little girl was standing to the side, with tears pouring down her face, and my partner walked straight past her and was asking shoppers, "Where is he?" When I pointed to the little girl, my officer looked at me dumbstruck. It was obvious that he had failed to process the information appropriately.

    As my officer was now dealing with the shopkeeper and the little girl, another officer walked in to the store, and I could tell that he was annoyed with something. What he was annoyed with was the way that my officer drove to this call, as it was clearly unacceptable. I will be honest here; I took the hit for my rookie, and simply stated that I had asked my driver to respond like it was a priority emergency call.

I can honestly say that I went home that night and was questioning my own actions. At the time, I wasn't aware of NRA, but I certainly knew that had something gone wrong, I would have felt responsible, knowing that I could have done something by intervening. This was the last time that I remained quiet during a ride-along. If I felt that I could help manage risk more effectively, I would begin my driver down this path: Is this style of driving necessary? "Yes…" Then, "No." (What changed? The information that the culp was an 11-year-old, crying for her mom.) Was this driving "risk effective?" "No." Was the driving acceptable? Judicially, yes; civilly and morally? NO!

Benefits of Incorporating NRA

I am sure that many of you could relate, in some small part, to my situation as we responded to the theft call. Perhaps it was when you were a rookie developing your own decision-making abilities, or perhaps when you were an FTO helping your rookie develop their decision making skills.

I know that EVO instructors spend time helping students to develop their decision-making, but we mostly rely on the rookies to garner this through experience. That doesn't seem like a great risk mitigation strategy to me. Wouldn't it make sense if we could get them to run it through the action criteria of NRA?

Ultimately, if something goes wrong, and people are asking our officers why they did what they did, wouldn't it be useful if they were able to articulate why they drove in the manner in which they did?

Yes, I agree that everyone makes mistakes, both the civilian drivers we encounter as well as our trained (professional) officers. Opposed to my situation that I encountered a dozen years ago, an appropriate application of the NRA criteria might look something more like this:

Necessary:

A shoplifting call comes in. Our particular agency's policy says that we are permitted to respond to this type of call, and deems it an emergency situation. The shop owner is requesting our services, and if we don't get there quickly, someone may get hurt. This could be the suspect, victim, or even a passerby. Therefore, it is deemed necessary that we respond to this call as a priority.

Risk Effective:

Are we driving in a risk effective manner? Have we activated all of our emergency equipment, given the fact that the roads are dry, we have good visibility, and traffic is relatively light? As well, there are no drivers intersecting our particular path of travel, and our speeds are higher but by no means are they near 100% of the posted speed limit. We actually stop and wait at the red traffic light, and we choose to switch off our emergency equipment and read the information on the computer. We learn that the 11- year-old suspect is crying for her mom, and there are no weapons present. Immediately, it is recognized that an emergency response—more specifically, proceeding against this red light—is not risk effective. Once you deem that an action is not risk effective, you can make changes to make it risk effective, at which point you move to acceptable.

Acceptable:

Asking if our driving is acceptable is not necessary in this particular scenario, as we didn't make it to stage three, because we already deemed that an emergency response was not risk effective. If, however, the information was slightly different, and we were not aware of the crying 11-year-old suspect, then it's possible that we would make it to the third stage of our action criteria: Is it acceptable?

Emergency Vehicle Operation Instruction

The process is in a continual loop and may change. Just like responding to an "officer needs assistance" call, at the outset, the call may be meeting the NRA action criteria, but it could change while we are enroute, i.e. other officers have arrived, and we are still 5 miles out—this no longer will stand the test of the NRA action criteria.

The introduction of the NRA action criteria model will undoubtedly assist officers with developing a strong decision making process, and will help them out over the duration of their career. This can easily be built into desktop exercises. Build three to five scenarios, and have the students apply the NRA action criteria, and then discuss what driving characteristics would be appropriate in each situation.

Not only does it help officers make effective decisions under stress, it could also help them to articulate their decisions in their notes, at an inquest, or at court. Often, it is not what the officer actually did but how they were able to articulate themselves months or years later. This model fills that gap.

Chapter 10

Training in Live Traffic

"Predictable is preventable."
– Gordon Graham

Driving – The Most Dangerous Thing

Over the history of law enforcement in North America, traditionally, line of duty deaths have been relatively balanced between felonious acts and motor vehicle-related fatalities. In 2019, that trend pretty much continued; if we removed the historical fatalities as a result of 9/11, firearms and assault make up for 41% of officer fatalities, and MVC related incidents were at 37%.

Obviously, driving a police vehicle is still a very dangerous task. Recently, I conducted a Workplace Injury survey at a local police service, and found that motor vehicle-related injuries ranked number three on the list, and was behind struggles with suspects/prisoners (#2), with the number #1 work-related incidents being slips and falls. The trend still continues well into 2020. As risk management expert, Gordon Graham, states, "If it's predictable, it's preventable." It's with this thought that I approach training of Emergency Vehicle Operators. A few years ago, a local news headline read, "It's Just Part of the Job," quoting a local police chief after one of his officers was killed in a MVC. No, this isn't part of the job! If we can get our people to make better decisions, drive at appropriate speeds, and buckle their seat belts, these fatalities can be prevented.

As professional EVO instructors, we have to adopt this philosophy when we are training our officers/drivers in the basic officer safety protocols.

If officers are going to be expected to drive on city streets and county roads without crashing their vehicles, perhaps we should train them in the exact same environment in which they will be working. I am fortunate that I have been training where the government acknowledges that training is part of an officer's duties, and therefore we train on city streets and roads. Why wouldn't you want new Emergency Vehicle Operators to be trained in a safe and controlled manner? With "safe" meaning to have an instructor onboard, and "controlled" meaning without the added pressure of attending an actual call.

When we are conducting training in live traffic, an EVO instructor must also be applying the NRA action criteria to the training session itself. Is it necessary for our student to be travelling at code, emergency mode for training? Why now? Traffic is considerably lighter, and the roads are dry, with excellent visibility. Is this training risk effective? My driver has progressed well to all previous training and has demonstrated a good understanding of the necessary skills and techniques. Is it acceptable? My supervisor is aware that I have used good judgment in getting my student to this position, and the community at large should expect that our officers are getting the best training possible. How better to train then to have them be observed by a trained instructor who may even have an auxiliary brake on their side of the vehicle.

The Aura of an Emergency Vehicle

Do you remember what it was like when you were first exposed to police and/or EMS motor vehicle operation? I remember the first ride along that I went on, and I couldn't get over just how different we were treated by all of the other road users just because we were in a fully marked police cruiser. I truly felt like I was in a fishbowl and everybody was watching—it took a great deal of time to get over that feeling of being watched. Just like you, I have become desensitized to that feeling, and just know that (fish bowl) is the consequence of being in a marked cruiser.

Do you remember when you first started driving a marked police vehicle, and arriving at an all-way stop sign? Being the second or maybe even the third vehicle to arrive, and yet the other traffic would not move until the police vehicle moved off? That is one of the easiest demonstrations to make to our students, to have them understand that the average road user reacts differently to police/EMS than other automobiles.

So far, we have discussed vehicles being operated at normal traffic speeds and without any of the emergency equipment activated. What happens when we have our driver activate the roof lights and the siren? Based on my experience, we have seen the vast majority of drivers (civilian traffic) appear to lose their proper thought process when they look into their mirror. That is, of course, if they actually are aware of our presence in the first place and actually look there.

Just take a moment and consider what happens inside the vehicle that is in front of an emergency vehicle with its lights and siren on. The driver and passengers are probably having a conversation about whatever is going on in their lives. It may be sports related, or political, or it could even be about the day-to-day happenings of a family—heck, there could even be a domestic happening inside! Fact is, we don't know, but what we do know is that they aren't thinking about their driving and/or how to get out of the way of an emergency vehicle. Inside the driver's head, it's business as usual as they carry on with life. On the other hand, what's going on inside of our heads? We are on our way to a call and are sending telepathic messages to the driver of the vehicle in front, asking them to look in the mirror, or more specifically, to get out of our way!

The first thing we have to do is just get the other driver's attention, and it feels like we need to get really close to them so that they can hear and/or see us. In actuality, getting closer is one of the worst things that we can do. The closer we get to them, the more difficult it is for them to see our roof lights. It also will become very emotional for that driver when they notice the emergency lights, resulting in their learned behaviour of slamming on the brakes. If we can just give them those 2 seconds of following distance, it will allow them to recognize our vehicle sooner, and more importantly, give them some time to process the information and decide how to move to where you want them to go. I always tell my students that *"you* know what to do when there's an emergency vehicle behind you"; however, most drivers haven't given it much thought since they first got their driver's license.

Speaking of following distances, awhile back I had an opportunity to ride with an officer who had been on the road for just over a year. During the first few hours of my ride-along, she made three different traffic stops. In all three, the driver ended up stopping in the left-most lane of 3. This was in the downtown core of a big city; however, traffic was moderate to light on this particular morning. When we later spoke about the drivers and them stopping in the fast lane, she said to me, "That always seems to happen on this road." She went on to say that she was open to receiving some tips to help avoid this from happening. As we drove, I suggested that we work on a minimum two seconds of following distance, and when she was about to activate the lights to affect a traffic stop, I suggested that she have the recommended following distance. The next traffic stop was near perfection; the driver made two lane changes and came to a stop on the right side of the road. Maybe that was just a high-level driver; let's try that again. The next stop was executed, and once again, the driver smoothly transitioned to the right-hand lane and came to a stop. We were two for two my way, and 0 for three hers! Hopefully, she became a believer, and this has become the norm for her traffic stops now.

Now let's get back to emergency runs. When the driver in front first notices the emergency vehicle behind them, a couple of different thoughts will run through their mind. If it is an ambulance or a fire truck, they will think that they need to get out of the way and let them go to the emergency. Okay, who's kidding who? They're probably thinking, "Oh my gosh, I don't want to have to end up behind them on the interstate," and then speed up. Overall, the majority of drivers will move out of the way. If, however, they look in the mirror and recognize the emergency vehicle to be a police car, their learned behaviour will be to check the speedometer and most likely go to the brake pedal simultaneously. If they are not speeding (in their minds), their mind immediately will start thinking that they're not doing anything wrong. This is the typical child thought pattern which we are all guilty of. Meanwhile the person operating the police vehicle is thinking; just get out of my way! Eventually the motorist will figure it out and (usually) move out of your way. It does however take some time for the driver to put everything cognitively together because it is not a simple reaction for them. We as professional instructors must help our students understand why it takes so long for some people to move out of the way of an emergency vehicle.

Feedback via Unsuspecting Motorists

Riding on board with a student when they begin their first emergency response drive can be a very rewarding experience. Okay, times it can be a little stressful but in reality that normally comes down to the way that I communicate with my driver. If they make some decisions that end up flustering themselves, I usually put that back on me as the instructor for failing to recognize they weren't ready for that particular manoeuvre/exercise.

When I say rewarding I mean that we can see the most Improvement during an emergency response training session. You can discuss all of the theories inside of a classroom and utilize video, whiteboards, and even case studies but it's quite a different animal when a student actually turns the lights and sirens on for the very first time. I am also a big fan of Dash cameras to review the student drives at a later time. This can afford me more time to ensure the student understands why we do certain things at certain times.

Earlier in this segment, we spoke about what is going on inside the other motorists head when they recognize an emergency vehicle's presence, so now let's discuss what goes on inside our student's heads when they activate the lights and sirens. First and foremost, they are going to get an adrenaline rush, which hopefully you have already discussed with your students. I think it is good for them to understand that it is normal to get this rush, especially at the beginning of their careers. I will sometimes review some strategies to help them manage this feeling, such as tactical breathing, proper scanning, and to keep moving their eyes to find potential hazards/surprises.

When practicing emergency runs in live traffic, I have found it important to allow my driver to make some decisions on their own, and would allow them to make some questionable decisions so that they can experience the consequences of their actions. Now, I'm not talking about just sitting idly by while they go through a red light without slowing or stopping, but I am referring to how they approach traffic with their emergency equipment on.

In most situations, during their first emergency drive, they will fixate on the bumper of the vehicle in front of them, thus being unable to plan further ahead, and most likely they will be traveling in the tire tracks of the vehicle in front. This is generally the time where I will ask them about something that is in the future, and encourage them to offset their vehicle to the left. Generally, the student will have experienced a few different learning moments during this time, and we will debrief them at the side of the road. Most likely, they will admit that they were fixated on the bumper of the car in front, and will usually be amazed by the fact that the vehicle in front pulled over to the right as soon as we offset our vehicle to the left. I will explain to my student that offsetting our vehicle provides a few benefits: It allows us to see further ahead; it indicates to the motorist ahead, of the path that you would like to take (on the left); and last but certainly not least, it allows the driver in front to have an unobstructed view in their mirror beyond your vehicle, thus allowing them an opportunity see that it's safe to move to the right and ultimately getting out of the way.

My drivers will encounter many other motorists who will provide good feedback to my student. Most notably, drivers will stop right in their lane without pulling over, which is most likely because my student has been too close to the vehicle in front of them. Other motorists will sometimes pull to the left as opposed to the right, which is normally a reaction to our emergency vehicle failing to indicate which way we would like to take past them.

Earlier, I mentioned about the officer making traffic stops, and in that particular case, it was not during a PVO training exercise but during a normal ride-along. For our purpose as an EVO instructor, a key component of our training should be conducting traffic stops. Many factors influence an officer's decision making, and at this point in the book, I hope that you are starting to apply the NRA action criteria model. Just because someone was speeding or rolled a stop sign, doesn't mean that it's *necessary* for an officer to make a traffic stop. During our traffic stop training sessions on the road it is imperative that we review NRA and have the student explain their Action criteria process. Sometimes we will allow the student to make the traffic stop in bad situations. By bad situations I am referring to heavy traffic, in front of driveways, near major intersections, or perhaps on the downside of the Hill. In all situations we as the instructors must way the benefits of having the student identify or deal with their poor choices well assessing the risk to ourselves and the public.

Training is much more beneficial when the student themselves recognizes that they made a bad decision and it's even better when they recognize it well working through the action criteria of NRA.

Training in the Real World

Throughout this book we have discussed the importance of proper eye placement, the advantages of commentary driving and the four stages of competency to name a few. When we move our training out into live traffic all of the previous components of this book are applied or more importantly come into play. We have already looked at the aura of a police vehicle and discussed what lessons our students can learn from other motorists. But you're probably wondering what training you actually do when you're out on the roadways. So, here are a few of them, and they are in no particular order.

- Basic safe driving, and monitoring the interactions with other road users
- Divided attention exercises, such as Q & A, and Follow Me exercise (mentioned earlier)
- Traffic stops
- Emergency response

Scenarios

My favourite PVO exercise is on-road scenario training. Scenario-based is a combination of all of the previously discussed strategies. Basically, we distract our students by giving them a call to attend, and their brain will be so preoccupied with processing all of the policing information that we will have an excellent opportunity to see what stage of competence their driving skills fall into. In a perfect world, we would see that the student is able to drive the vehicle at the unconscious competent level. That, however, is unrealistic considering that many of the skills necessary have just been introduced to them in previous training. We expect to see them stepping in and out of stage two and three during scenario day.

So what does that look like, you are thinking? There are numerous scenarios with which we can put our students into, but it all comes down to what we want the learning outcomes to be. If it is just vehicle identification and traffic stops that you want to review, design your scenario with that in mind. An example of that might be to locate a vehicle and give out a description with or without the license plate of the vehicle. He has just committed a minor offense, such as a theft of gas. As the student proceeds towards the area, we would have them be running this call through NRA. Hopefully, the student will not feel the need to race there, by understanding that this type of call isn't necessary to get there quickly, and hopefully they will actually be slowing down so that they can see more, with the hopes of locating the suspect vehicle.

Perhaps he/she will notice the suspect vehicle (driven by another instructor), and this will give us an opportunity to see how they process this information and apply it to his/her drive. Is it necessary to go through this red light; is it risk effective; will their actions acceptable? Once the student locates the vehicle, how do they perform the traffic stop? Does it meet policy and procedure and your standards for technique?

This one little scenario will allow you to evaluate your student's driving within all of the aspects of your training. How was the basic drive and interaction with other motorists? Was there scanning? Perhaps we even asked them to do a commentary drive while they were looking for the suspect vehicle. Was their driving appropriate for the call, and how was your student's application of NRA? How was your student's application of your policies and procedures?

Another scenario, which is one of my favourites and truly allows the student to apply their knowledge of your organization's policy and directives, as well as the NRA, is the BOLO broadcast for a suspect vehicle that has been involved in a pursuit from another jurisdiction. For this particular scenario, the expectation is that once the vehicle has been spotted, and our student runs it through the service policy and NRA, they will most likely not pursue. However, it is very interesting to have them reflect back when they are in the classroom, and say that they would not engage in a pursuit for a trivial matter, and yet here in the scenario, he/she very quickly wanted to pursue. By the way, we will sometimes give our student the reason that the other jurisdiction was in pursuit, and it is often for a theft of gas.

Truth be told, we have many scenarios with which to draw upon, and it always comes down to what the learning outcomes are. We have a scenario for alarm calls, shop theft, assault, motor vehicle crashes, all the way up to an officer needing assistance. In the majority of these scenarios, we are looking at the decision making of our students, and the application of our policies and procedures. These scenarios aren't meant to be pass or fail, but more like experiences from which they can draw upon in the future.

Timely Instructor Communication

Throughout this book, we have discussed many different strategies and tips for enhancing your EVO training. In truth, it's not always the *what* or the *why,* but it sometimes comes down to the *how*. Don't get me wrong; I believe the primary role of an EVO instructor is to train our students as to the *why*. I believe that if someone understands *why* we do something, they will be better placed to incorporate whatever technique and/or strategy we are discussing, into their portfolio. If a child understands why they shouldn't touch a hot stove, because they will get burned, then there is a much higher probability that they will not touch a hot stove. So, in general terms, the *how* we do things is often left up to the field training officers, and the professional instructors handle the *whys*.

Let's now switch our mindset to the instructor's perspective. Why is it important that an instructor communicate clearly with their students? So that we can mitigate risk to all parties, including the student, ourselves, and perhaps most importantly, the general public.

I have had a few occasions where I had failed to communicate clearly with my student. During a very simple drive, I asked my driver to go through the stop, and we would pull into the parking lot on the right. I clearly expected my driver to stop for the stop sign, and then once safe, we would proceed through and into the parking lot; however, my driver didn't take it that way. He simply drove through the stop sign without slowing and proceeded to turn into the parking lot. We were fortunate that no cross traffic was present, but it could have been a different situation. I will always preface that instruction with: Once we stop at the stop sign, and it is safe to do so, we will proceed through to the parking lot. I'm not kidding; every time I drive down there, I now think of this moment. What's that saying about "once bitten, twice shy?"

Doing scenarios one day, we had a student who failed to engage in our little exercise. The expectation was for my driver to see the other vehicle, which was being operated by another instructor, and once that vehicle was spotted, we would conduct a U-turn and catch up to that vehicle, and then provide license plate detail prior to conducting a traffic stop on said vehicle. Now, before I go any further, I will provide you with just a little background tennis exercise. My partner and I at the time had probably conducted this exercise with 40 to 50 officers over the previous couple of years, and we couldn't understand why our driver wasn't giving us the typical results.

I was pretty certain that our driver had seen me on every pass, which was about 3 times. My partner and I pulled into a parking lot to debrief, and when we asked the student why she had been engaged with the suspect vehicle, she simply stated "because it wasn't the right car." And yet she admitted that she had seen me pass her on each and every occasion.

What had happened was when I broadcasted the make and model of the suspect vehicle, I did it from memory and said that they were looking for a grey Chevrolet Impala, which is my normal car for this exercise; however, on today's date, that car was in the shop, and I was driving a black Dodge Charger. Unfortunately, both my partner and I didn't recognize that I was giving the wrong description, because we were so used to the description always being a grey Chevrolet Impala. Oops, no one is perfect.

Now, the previous two examples were very minor in nature and certainly didn't cause a great deal of risk to the general public or ourselves. However, you can imagine that the potential for risk is far greater once we start conducting emergency response training. Generally, I can say that we don't fall into too many traps during this training; because we are all hyper vigilant. Clear instructions prior to the exercise, the student having already witnessed a demonstration drive from an instructor, along with the radical discussion in the classroom, will precede any on-road training.

The major risk that could occur would be where an instructor is trying to push their student into a situation where the student is not yet comfortable. Just because the instructor has a very high level of risk homeostasis, doesn't mean that their student is at such a level. Sometimes we are all guilty of trying to get our students to drive like us. During an emergency drive, this can lead to disaster, and therefore it is imperative that if a student isn't comfortable with something, then the instructor must acquiesce and bring that component of training to a safe halt. If a student has already made a mental decision to stop for a light that is going from green to red, there is no sense in the instructor telling them to go through it! The delay within the cognitive processes puts all parties at risk. During training, there are no real downsides to stopping for a red light.

It is important for an EVO instructor to recognize what level of risk homeostasis they operate at. Basically, risk homeostasis means the amount of risk that you find acceptable within your life and well-being, and understand that every individual operates at a different level. How does that affect an EVO instructor, you might ask? There's no sense in trying to train a student to drive just like us. Our goal should be to give them the knowledge, skills, and attitude that will help them evolve into becoming the best emergency vehicle operations driver that they can be. As a colleague of mine has often said to his students, if you drive following the state/provincial traffic rules, and within the policies and procedures of your organization, and adhere to the EVO training, you're within the circle of protection should something happen to go wrong. However, once you step outside any of those three circles, you will not be protected.

Epilogue

If you made it this far in the book, you have realised that this wasn't a "how-to" book, in the true sense of the word. Although there was a smattering of "how-to" throughout, the real purpose of this book was to open up your mind to other concepts within driver training. I'm sure that you have heard of some of these concepts before, and may have already incorporated them into your current training. It was my hope to expand your mind as to what other training is available, and how it can help you become the best EVO instructor that you can be. When you picked this book up, you probably expected to find a sequential 5-step plan, because you noticed the subtitle, "Five Steps to Enhance Your EVOC Training." In my mind, these five steps are located within a garden of knowledge that you already possess. You will now take these techniques and place one or all five of them in and amongst your pre-existing knowledge and experience. Perhaps you are looking to incorporate commentary driving into your simulator training program, while others will be anxious to expand on the Eye Placement training within their track work. Depending on your place within the garden, will dictate where your next step should be.

I'm sure that many of you have already been practicing the four stages of competence at some sort of level. You may not have broken it down quite to the same degree that was discussed in Chapter 6, but you probably had a good understanding of stages number one and two. Hopefully, you will now introduce the four stages of competency to the student, and help them understand the process of moving from unconscious, or basically not knowing what you don't know, and then transitioning to the ultimate goal of unconscious competency, where you don't even think about it anymore, and it's just on autopilot.

I'm sure that many of you understand the benefits of proper eye placement and have already incorporated it into your cone and track training. I hope that after reading this, I will have enhanced your understanding a little bit, and given you some clues as to how you can help draw the correlation between track training and driving on the road. Now point your drivers to success, with strategies on how they can practice daily.

Commentary driving is my favourite strategy because it has consistently shown the most benefits within all of my years of training. It will work for you too. I know that some trainers have incorporated this into simulator training, and I can see this being very beneficial, but I also know that it works well during track training as well. I challenge you to get your driver's to conduct/practice a commentary even when they are by themselves. It will undoubtedly help them become expert scanners and, ultimately, a very proficient Emergency Vehicle Operator.

For many years now, we have been throwing around the term, "getting driver's to make better decisions." In fact, I have even been known to use that term myself—even earlier inside this book. How do we go about helping drivers make better decisions? Hopefully, you will agree that incorporating the NRA action criteria into our training can help them with this process. Getting drivers to incorporate NRA will also help them outside of the motor vehicle. It could be of benefit when answering some basic questions that often seem to come about after a high-risk situation: Why did you do what you did? Why then? What changed? Was there a less risky option, and was your decision acceptable to your supervisor, civilly or judiciously? However, I will leave that to people who are much smarter than I.

I know that the most controversial chapter within this book will be the component on training in live traffic. I want you to ask yourself: If we continue to do things the way we always have, won't we continue to get the same results? If we want different results, we will have to do things differently. Do you want different results? You may have to take on the fight of the importance of having training on the streets, and not be confined to some back parking lot with hundreds of orange cones. It may take baby steps, but every step toward training in live traffic will be more beneficial to our students. Perhaps it will only mean doing commentary driving with regular road users, but for many jurisdictions, that will be a great start.

If this book has caused you to stop and rethink some of your training—awesome, it did its job. If it made you pause to learn some of the theories in here—awesome, it did its job. If, however, the book caused you to evaluate what you do, and this book validated what you are already doing—awesome, it did its job.

I hope that this book has inspired you to enhance your EVO training at all levels, and that your thirst for knowledge will continue. Check out evoctrainor.com for updated information and/or for any upcoming professional development workshops. Please be safe, and remember to keep the shiny side up.

www.ingramcontent.com/pod-product-compliance
Lightning Source LLC
Chambersburg PA
CBHW050829160426
43192CB00010B/1961